Adrian Goldsworthy was awarded a doctorate in ancient history by Oxford University and has taught at a number of universities. His many published works, which have been translated into more than a dozen languages, include the critically acclaimed *Caesar: The Life of a Colossus* and most recently *The Fall of the West: The Death of the Roman Superpower*. A full-time author, he has also written the novel *True Soldier Gentlemen*, the first in a series following the fortunes of a group of British soldiers in the fight against Napoleon. He is currently a Visiting Fellow at the University of Newcastle. Visit his website at www.adriangoldsworthy.com

CANNAE

ADRIAN GOLDSWORTHY

PHOENIX

Previous page:
This Roman
copy of a famous
Hellenistic statue
depicts a dying
Gallic warrior. The
original was part
of a monument
commemorating
the victory
of the King of
Pergamum over
the Gallic or
Galatian tribes
of Asia Minor
earlier in the
third century BC.

A PHOENIX PAPERBACK

First published in Great Britain in 2001
by Cassell & Co
This paperback edition published in 2007
by Phoenix,
an imprint of Orion Books Ltd,
Orion House, 5 Upper St Martin's Lane
London WC2H 9EA

10 9 8 7 6 5 4 3 2

Copyright © Adrian Goldsworthy, 2001
Foreword © Richard Holmes, 2001

The right of Adrian Goldsworthy to be identified as the author
of this work has been asserted by him in accordance with the
Copyright, Designs & Patents Act 1988.

A CIP catalogue record for this book is available from the British Library.

ISBN 978-0-7538-2259-3

Printed and bound in China

The Orion Publishing Group's policy is to use papers that are natural, renewable and
recyclable products and made from wood grown in sustainable forests. The logging
and manufacturing processes are expected to conform to the environmental regula-
tions of the country of origin.

www.orionbooks.co.uk

CONTENTS

Acknowledgements   7

Foreword by Richard Holmes   9

Introduction   13

1 CARTHAGE, ROME AND THE PUNIC WARS   17

The Second Punic War   22

Hannibal Barca   24

Invasion, 218–217 BC   28

'The Delayer', Summer to Autumn 217 BC   37

2 RIVAL ARMIES   41

The Roman Military System   41

The Carthaginian Military System and Hannibal's Army   50

3 THE CAMPAIGN OF 216 BC   59

The Leaders   60

The Led   64

The Plan   70

The Campaign   74

4 **THE BATTLE OF CANNAE, 2 AUGUST 216 BC**   83

Locating the Battlefield   86

Initial Deployment   95

The Battle

   Opening Moves   113

   The Cavalry Clash on the Wings   118

   The Roman Centre Advances   127

   The Charge to Contact   132

   Encirclement   143

   Annihilation   150

5 **THE AFTERMATH**   157

Mopping Up   157

How to Use a Victory   160

The Long Struggle, 216–201 BC   168

Cannae in History   176

Notes   180

Appendix 1: Numbers   188

Appendix 2: Casualties   192

Glossary   195

ACKNOWLEDGEMENTS

Many family members and friends contributed to the final form of this book. I must pay particular thanks once again to Ian Hughes who read and commented on successive versions of the manuscript. Others who greatly enhanced the clarity of the final text include Dr Hugh Deeks and Averil Goldsworthy. Conversations over several years and with many other people have helped to modify and refine my ideas about the battle itself and the nature of combat in this period. There are too many to mention them all, but I ought to thank in particular Professor Philip Sabin and Dr Louis Rawlings.

In addition, I must thank the Series Editor, Professor Richard Holmes, for his thought provoking comments on an earlier draft of the text. Finally, praise should also go to Keith Lowe for his continued efforts.

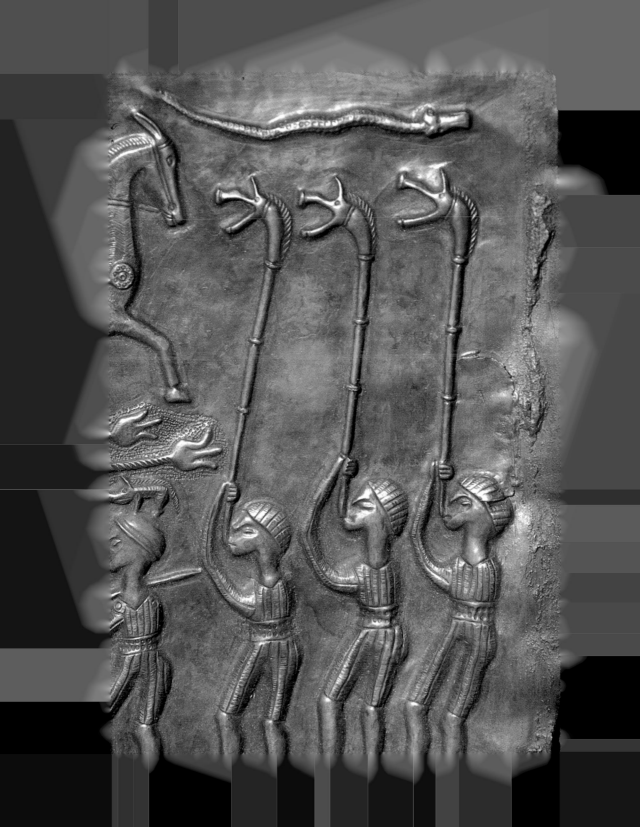

FOREWORD

Cannae is more than just a battle. True, the scale of its slaughter – Adrian Goldsworthy is right to call it 'one of the bloodiest single day's fighting in history', when the Romans lost more men killed than the British army on the first day of the Somme in 1916 – and the brilliance of Hannibal's generalship makes it a remarkable one. But its resonance spread far beyond classical Italy, and Cannae, the supreme model of the destruction of a superior force by an inferior one, became an ideal striven after by many commanders. Count Alfred von Schlieffen, chief of the German General Staff from 1891 to 1906, argued that if Germany was to fight a two-front war 'ordinary' victories were no help to her: she had to win a battle of annihilation. He was fascinated by Cannae: a collection of his writings was published under the title Cannae in 1925.

The Schlieffen plan strove to achieve the strategic envelopment of the French, with the armies of the German right wing swinging round to snap in behind their opponents. If the French persisted in attacking into the 'lost provinces' of Alsace and Lorraine (just the numerically superior Roman infantry bit deep into Hannibal's centre at Cannae) they would simply be doing the Germans 'a kindly favour', and make their own ultimate defeat more certain. The battles of encirclement won by the Germans on the Eastern Front in 1941 were 'super-Cannaes' on a shocking scale, and General Norman H. Schwarzkopf's plan for the 1990-91 Gulf War was based on Hannibal's concept.

However, like so many battles of ancient and medieval history, where sources are generally incomplete and archaeological evidence is often scanty,

Celtic warriors depicted on the Gunderstrup cauldron found in Denmark and dating to the first century BC. Each man blows a tall trumpet (carnyx) which was said to produce a particularly harsh noise. The Gauls serving in Hannibal's army at Cannae probably looked little different to these men and almost certainly used the carnyx.

Cannae is a clash which has generated more than its fair share of speculation. Adrian Goldsworthy has made a major contribution to our understanding in three distinct respects. Firstly, by his description of the contending forces, using original sources reinforced by the best of recent scholarship. For example, he notes Polybius's comments on the use of heavy and light pila (the Roman throwing spear) but observes that archaeological evidence suggests rather more variety. And he warns against fanciful descriptions of how Roman infantry formations might have closed up from the relatively open quincunx pattern (like the five on a die) just before contact, pointing out that 'there is not a shred of evidence from our sources to support them.' The same principle – painstaking analysis of original sources weighed against military logic – also inspires his careful discussion of the battlefield. Its exact location is a source of controversy, and his discussion of possible sites supports Peter Connolly's suggestion that the fighting actually took place just north of the hills around the town of Cannae.

Lastly, in his description of the combat Adrian Goldsworthy follows the methodology of John Keegan's seminal work The Face of Battle, which was applied to combat in classical Greece by Victor D. Hanson in The Western Way of War, in a penetrating description of what really happened when men hewed and stabbed at one another in sweaty and breathless close combat. His analysis of the Roman centre at Cannae, where an exceptionally large number of men were formed up on a very narrow frontage, emphasises the psychological benefits conferred by such a formation, especially on inexperienced or patchily-trained troops.

The Roman plan was 'simple and unsubtle, but not unreasonable or by any means inevitably doomed to failure.' It emphasised Roman affection for what Polybius termed 'brute force' and, because it would rely on the flanking cavalry holding on long enough for the infantry to win the battle in the centre, it explains the fact that Varro and Paullus, the Roman consuls, positioned themselves with the cavalry on the flanks. Roman generals 'tended to station themselves wherever they could most influence the battle and thus usually where they anticipated its crisis to occur, hence the consuls' presence with the cavalry at Cannae.' Hannibal's plan, in contrast, was complex, and made heavy demands on his soldiers. Hannibal also positioned himself at what he saw as the decisive point: in his centre, where his Spaniards and Gauls had to hang on to let the cavalry on the wings complete the encirclement of the Roman army.

Adrian Goldsworthy first considers the battle between the opposing skirmishers, suggesting that, as was so often the case, it inflicted relatively few casualties, although the superior quality of Hannibal's light troops balanced Roman numerical superiority. He then goes on to examine the cavalry battles on the flanks, where Hannibal's men had the better of things, especially on the Roman right, where Hasdrubal quickly beat his opponents and was soon ready to enter the infantry battle. The Roman infantry attack was prepared by an exchange of missiles before the ranks met with an audible clash. There then followed a period with 'the two front ranks separated by a metre or so, prodding and cutting at each other' to produce the characteristic wound-pattern of injuries to the lower leg, the right arm and the left side of the head. Once a man was brought down he would be finished off with a heavy blow to the head. Despite the brave performance of Hannibal's Gallic and Spanish infantry, the weight of numbers proved too much, and as they broke they suffered heavy losses, and the Romans, their ranks now disordered, pressed forward in pursuit.

But as Hannibal's centre at last collapsed, he committed his fresh Libyan infantry against both flanks of the victorious Roman centre, gripping it like a vice while the Carthaginian cavalry swung in against the Roman rear. Most accounts now conclude, simply observing that the encircled Romans were annihilated. But Adrian Goldsworthy dissects this final phase of the battle as well as he has its earlier elements, reminding us of the grinding physical effort involved in hand to hand fighting with edged weapons, and pointing to the sporadic nature the battle, with local lulls and rallies. He points out that the cost of victory was heavy for Hannibal: fixing a determined opponent to allow time for decisive strikes to be mounted against his vulnerable points is often an expensive business.

If victory was expensive, defeat was exorbitant: the Romans lost around 50,000 men killed. Hannibal did not move rapidly on Rome after his victory, for a variety of reasons, like exhaustion, reluctance to embark upon a lengthy siege and, most significantly, the expectation that Rome would behave like most other city-states under such circumstances and sue for peace. She did not, and although the balance of the war was tilted in Hannibal's favour – most of southern Italy defected to him – he was never able to mint strategic victory from his tactical success. Nor were so many of his subsequent imitators. For a victory like Cannae need not prove conclusive provided the loser retains the political and popular resolve to fight on: the dream of Cannae has too often become a nightmare.

RICHARD HOLMES

INTRODUCTION

On 2 August 216BC the Carthaginian General Hannibal won one of the most complete battlefield victories in history. Outnumbered nearly two to one, his heterogeneous army of Africans, Spaniards and Celts not merely defeated, but virtually destroyed the Roman army opposing them. By the end of the day, nearly 50,000 Roman and Allied soldiers lay dead or were dying in an area of a few square kilometres, whilst between ten and twenty thousand more were prisoners. Less than 20% of one of the largest armies ever fielded by the Roman State survived to reform over the next few weeks. Cannae became the yardstick by which the Romans measured later catastrophes, but only one or two defeats in their history were ever judged to have been as bad. The scale of the losses at Cannae was unrivalled until the industrialised slaughter of the First World War.

Most battles from the Ancient World are now all but forgotten, for military as well as civil education has ceased to be based fundamentally on the Classics. Yet Cannae is still regularly referred to in the training programmes of today's army officers. Hannibal's tactics appear almost perfect, the classic example of double envelopment, and ever since many commanders have attempted to reproduce their essence and their overwhelming success. Nearly all have failed. Cannae was the largest in a series of defeats Hannibal inflicted on the Romans, but, though he never lost a major engagement in Italy, eventually he was forced to evacuate his army and Carthage lost the war. The genius of his tactics at Cannae should not obscure the stages of the battle when things could easily have gone the other way and a great Roman victory resulted.

Hannibal won the battle through not only his dynamic leadership and the high quality of his army, but also because of a good deal of luck. Cannae was not an exercise in pure tactics, but, like all battles, a product both of the military doctrines and technology of the time and the peculiar circumstances of a specific campaign.

The aim of this book is to place Cannae firmly within the perspective of the Second Punic War and the nature of warfare in the third century BC. The events of this period are poorly recorded in comparison with more recent conflicts, and no official documents survive from either side for the Cannae campaign. Instead we have the narratives of historians, written anytime from seventy to several hundred years after the events they describe. Frequently these sources contradict one another, or fail to tell us things we would wish to know, and so there are many aspects of the campaign and battle which cannot be reconstructed with absolute certainty. Two accounts provide us with the greater part of our information and it is worth briefly considering these.

The earliest and best was written by the Greek historian Polybius in the second half of the second century BC. Polybius was a one of a group of hostages sent to Rome after the Third Macedonian War (172-168BC). He became an intimate of Scipio Aemilianus, the grandson of one of the Roman commanders at Cannae, following him on campaign in the Third Punic War (149-6BC) and witnessing the final destruction of Carthage. Polybius produced a *Universal History* describing events throughout the Mediterranean down until his own day, and its main theme was to explain for Greek audiences how Rome had so quickly emerged as the dominant world power. His narrative is generally sober and analytical, and he provides us with by far the best description of the Roman army. However, whilst willing to criticise the Romans in general, he is invariably sympathetic to all of the ancestors by blood or adoption of Scipio Aemilianus. Polybius' account survives intact for the battle itself, but then breaks off and only small fragments survive for the remaining years of the war.

The other main account was written in Latin by Livy in the late first century BC as part of his *History of Rome from the Foundation of the City*. His narrative is fiercely patriotic, stylistically elegant and intensely dramatic, but far less critically rigorous than that of Polybius. Livy used the Greek historian as one of his sources, but also drew upon a range of other traditions, most very favourable to the Romans and many celebrating the deeds of particular aristocratic families. He is useful because he provides information about some things, for instance Roman elections and politics, which are passed over very briefly by Polybius. In addition Livy's narrative survives intact for the entire Second Punic War, making him our main source for the aftermath of the battle.

Other sources provide some additional information, but all were written considerably later. Appian wrote a Roman history around the turn of the first and second centuries AD, but his account of Cannae makes very little sense and is of dubious reliability. Around the same time, Plutarch produced a collection of biographical *Lives*, some of which include accounts of the period. Such late sources need to be used with extreme caution, but it is possible that they preserved a few accurate details absent from the surviving portions of our earlier sources.

Cannae today: the stone ruins here date to a later period, when the town was rebuilt.

A t the start of the third century BC the Republic of Carthage was the wealthiest and most powerful state in the Western Mediterranean. It had been founded, probably in the late eighth century, by Phoenician settlers from Tyre on the coast of modern-day Lebanon. The Phoenicians were the great maritime traders of the ancient world – the Romans knew them as '*Poeni*', hence Punic – and eventually Carthage came to control trade in the West, dominating the coasts of Africa and Spain as well as Sicily, Sardinia, Corsica and the lesser islands of the region. The scientific exploitation of the then fertile agricultural land of North Africa combined with the profits of trade to make the city fabulously rich. However, this wealth was not evenly distributed and remained almost entirely in the hands of the small number of Carthaginian citizens, and especially the aristocracy. Preserving their Semitic language, religion and culture, and jealously guarding the

View of the remains of great Circular Harbour at Carthage. This inner harbour was reserved for military use, and included ramps for 180 quinqueremes or 'fives', the standard warship of the third-second centuries BC.

privileges of citizenship, the descendants of the Punic settlers remained a distinct élite. In contrast the indigenous population, especially the Libyans, were heavily taxed, exploited as agricultural labour and military manpower, and had no real share in the profits of empire.

Until 265 BC Rome remained a purely Italian power, and had by this time subjugated all of the Peninsula south of the River Po. From very early in their history the Romans displayed a remarkable talent for absorbing others. Enemies defeated in war became subordinate allies and in future supplied men and material for the next generation of Rome's wars. The Romans were unique in the ancient world in their willingness to grant citizenship to outsiders. Some former enemies became full citizens or citizens with limited rights, whilst others were granted the lesser rights of Latins, each grade being a legal status, rather than reflecting actual ethnic and linguistic distinctions. Each community was tied directly to Rome in a treaty which made clear both its rights and its obligations. The allies helped to fight Rome's wars and shared, at least to a limited extent, in their profits. As Rome expanded its population grew. The total land owned by Carthaginian and Roman citizens respectively in 265 BC was probably roughly equivalent in size, but the numbers of the former were tiny in comparison to the latter. The obligation of all citizens and allies possessing a minimum property qualification to serve in Rome's armies gave the Republic immense reserves of military manpower.[1]

In 265 BC the Romans for the first time sent an army overseas, when an expedition responded to an appeal to intervene in the affairs of a Sicilian city. Carthage, who had long possessed a presence in the island, even if it had never managed to subjugate it completely, resented this intrusion and responded with force. The result was the First Punic War (264–241 BC), an arduous struggle fought on a far bigger scale than either side could have imagined when they so lightly entered the conflict. The war was mainly fought in and around Sicily, with the most important battles occurring at sea, where fleets of hundreds of oared warships clashed in confused, swirling mêlées. In 256 the Romans invaded Africa and threatened Carthage itself, but the initial willingness of the Punic authorities to seek peace withered when faced with what they considered to be extremely harsh Roman demands. The Carthaginians fought on, and managed to destroy the Roman expeditionary force in battle, winning their only major victory on land in the entire war. In the naval war the Punic fleet proved unable to turn its greater experience to tangible advantage, losing all but one of the major battles. Losses were appalling on both sides, the Romans losing hundreds of ships to bad weather, although relatively few to enemy action. In the last years of the

Next page:
The Mediterranean World in 218 BC was divided into many different states and kingdoms. In the West Carthage still controlled North Africa and parts of Spain, although it had lost Sicily, Sardinia and Corsica to Rome after the First Punic War. In Northern Italy, Spain, Gaul, and Illyricum many small, but warlike tribal groups fought each other and their neighbours. The Eastern Mediterranean reflected the fragmentation of Alexander the Great's vast Empire with three main Kingdoms emerging in Syria, Egypt and Macedonia as well as many smaller communities. By the middle of the next century the entire Mediterranean would be dominated by Rome.

The Mediterranean World in 218 BC

Carthaginian territory

Roman territory

0   100   200 Miles
0 100 200   Km

Black   Sea

*atic
Sea*

Brundisium
●
● Tarentum

aclea

● Croton

Locri
um

Charax
●

M a c e d o n i a

● Apollonia

T h r a c e

B i t h y n i a

P o n t u s

G a l a t i a

P h r y g i a

P e r g a m u m

*S e l e u c i d
E m p i r e*

A e t o l i a

L y d i a

Athens
●

A r c a d i a

C a r i a

L y c i a

M e d i t e r r a n e a n   S e a

Alexandria
●

Cairo
●

*P t o l e m a i c
E g y p t*

war both sides were close to utter exhaustion, their treasuries drained by the costs of maintaining the struggle. In 241 BC a Roman fleet, paid for largely by voluntary loans made by individuals to the state, defeated the last Punic fleet at the battle of the Aegates Islands. Carthage no longer had the resources to continue the struggle and had no choice but to accept peace on terms dictated by Rome, giving up her last territory and influence in Sicily and paying a heavy indemnity.[2]

THE SECOND PUNIC WAR

The peace between Rome and Carthage lasted almost as long as the First War. From the very beginning some Carthaginians resented the surrender and believed it to be unnecessary. Foremost amongst these was Hamilcar Barca, the commander of the army in Sicily, who for nearly a decade had waged a war of skirmishes, raid and ambush with the Romans. Hamilcar had never fought a pitched battle, and his victories over the Romans were small in scale, but he believed, or affected to believe, that he could have continued to fight for years, and perhaps eventually worn the enemy down. Resigning his command in a public display of disgust at the surrender, he left others to disband his merce-nary army. The task was botched, and the mercenaries first mutinied and then rebelled, taking much of the Libyan population with them, for Carthaginian rule, always harsh, had become especially burdensome as they struggled to fund the war with Rome. The resulting Mercenary War was fought with appalling cruelty by both sides and came very close to destroying Carthage. In the end it was ruthlessly suppressed by Hamilcar in a series of campaigns which demonstrated his skill as a commander far more clearly than had the fighting in Sicily during the war with Rome.

The Romans honoured the treaty and did not at first exploit the weakness of their former enemy, rejecting appeals for an alliance from Carthage's rebel-lious allies. However, in the closing stages of the rebellion, they seized Sardinia and threatened a renewal of war if Carthage resisted. The Roman action was blatantly cynical and emphasized just how far Carthaginian power had declined since their defeat. More than anything else, this added to the deep sense of humiliation and resentment felt by much of the population. In 237 Hamilcar Barca was given command of the Carthaginian province in Spain and immediately began a programme of expansion. Some areas, especially those containing valuable mineral deposits, were taken under direct rule, whilst others were brought under Punic influence. All of the campaigns and diplomacy were carried out by members of the Barcid family. When Hamilcar was killed in battle in 229, he was succeeded by his son-in-law, Hasdrubal, who in turn was followed by Hamilcar's son Hannibal in 221. It is now hard to know how much independence the Barcids enjoyed in Spain, so that they have been variously depicted as loyal servants obeying the instructions of the Punic authorities and as semi-independent Hellenistic princes. Expansion in Spain brought great wealth – the coins minted in considerable numbers by the Barcids have an especially high silver content – and increased access to the fertile recruiting ground offered by the warlike Spanish tribes. The campaigns to achieve this expansion helped to create the nucleus of a highly efficient army, hardened by long experience of fighting under familiar officers. Once again, it is difficult to know to what extent these benefits were to the Republic as a whole, or served to further the ambitions of Hamilcar and his family.

The Romans viewed the growth of Punic power in Spain with great suspicion. In 226 BC a Roman embassy forced Hasdrubal to agree to a treaty barring Carthage from expanding beyond the River Ebro. The border of the Punic province was still some way south of the river and thus this was not an especially harsh measure, but it demonstrated the Romans' belief that they were free to impose restrictions on their former enemy whenever they wished. The treaty placed no restriction at all on Roman activity. In 220 Hannibal supported one of the tribes allied to Carthage in a dispute with the city of Saguntum. This was south of the Ebro, but at some point had become an ally of Rome, to whom the Saguntines swiftly appealed for protection. The Romans sent an embassy to instruct Hannibal to abandon his siege of the city, probably expecting him to back down as the Carthaginians had always done in the past. Hannibal continued the assault and finally captured Saguntum in 219 BC after an eight month siege, sacking it and enslaving the population. The Romans protested to Carthage and, when the authorities there refused to condemn Hannibal and hand him over for punishment, declared war at the beginning of 218 BC.[3]

HANNIBAL BARCA

A bust which may be a representation of Hannibal in later life, although there are no definite images of him. At Cannae he was still in his twenties, although he had already lost the use of one eye. In the same way that his appearance is uncertain, there is much about Hannibal's character which eludes us and, for all his achievements, he remains an enigmatic figure.

Hannibal was in his late twenties when he led his army out from his base at New Carthage to begin the Italian expedition in the spring of 218 BC. He was already an experienced soldier, having accompanied the army on campaign under his father and brother-in-law, serving in a variety of increasingly senior roles as soon as he was old enough. Since his elevation to the command in Spain in 221, he had already begun to display the speed of action, tactical genius and inspirational leadership which were subsequently to dazzle his Roman opponents. Our sources tell us a good deal about what Hannibal actually did, allowing us to appreciate his extraordinary talent, but provide little reliable information about his character. No source has survived written from the Carthaginian perspective, although we know that at least two Greek scholars, one of them Hannibal's tutor the Spartan Sosylus, accompanied his army and recorded its campaigns. Hannibal had some knowledge of Greek culture and history, but it is unclear how important a part this played in his life or to what extent he remained firmly the product of his own Semitic culture.[4]

The Roman and Greek authors, who wrote in a world dominated by Rome, were sure that a deep hatred of Rome was fundamental to Hannibal's character throughout his life. Polybius tells us that in the 190s BC, whilst an exile at the court of the Seleucid King Antiochus III, Hannibal told the monarch how his father had taken him to sacrifice at the temple of Ba'al Shamin before leaving for Spain in 237. Hamilcar asked the 9 year-old boy whether he wished

to come with him to Spain, and then, when the lad had eagerly begged for the chance to go, led him to the altar and made him swear a solemn oath 'never to be a friend to the Romans'. The story reaches us at best third hand, and was told by the Carthaginian to reassure Antiochus that he was not secretly meeting with Roman agents. As a result it is now impossible to know whether or not it is true, but the Romans certainly believed that the main cause of the Second Punic War was the enmity of Hamilcar and his sons. Only Hamilcar's death prevented him from completing the revival of Carthage's military power and launching an invasion of Italy from Spain, but the project continued to be the main ambition of his family and reached fulfilment under his eldest son.[5]

Debate continues to rage over the real causes of the Second Punic War, but need not concern us here. What is clear is that, whether or not the war was premeditated, Hannibal had developed a definite plan for how to fight Rome and had spent years preparing for this. In the spring of 218 BC he was able to lead out an enormous army, allegedly consisting of 12,000 cavalry, 90,000 infantry and 37 elephants, to begin a march which would take him across the River Ebro, over the Pyrenees, through Gaul and finally across the Alps into Italy. The First Punic War had been fought largely in Sicily and, although they had raided the Italian coast, the Carthaginians had never struck at the enemy's heartland as the Romans had done when they invaded Africa in 256 BC. Throughout the conflict the Carthaginians had remained remarkably passive, reacting to Roman moves but seldom initiating a major offensive. Their strategy was based on enduring the Roman onslaughts, persevering in their resistance in the hope that the enemy would become tired and then either withdraw or be vulnerable to attack. This approach had worked in the past, wearing down successive tyrants and mercenary leaders hired by the Greeks of Sicily. It failed against the Romans, who consistently returned to the offensive even after serious defeats, and who were both able and willing to devote massive resources to the war.[6]

Hannibal intended to fight the new war with Rome in a far bolder fashion than the First Punic War. Preparations were made to defend his Spanish base

The Second Punic War was provoked by Hannibal's capture of the city of Saguntum after an eight-month siege. Saguntum (modern Sagunto in Spain) was subsequently rebuilt and flourished during the Roman period when this monumental theatre was constructed. The theatre and other parts of the Ancient buildings were later incorporated into the town's medieval defences.

and Carthage's North African heartland against attack, but the main effort would be an offensive striking directly at the centre of Roman power in Italy itself. This time the Carthaginians would not attempt simply to endure enemy attacks, but would escalate the conflict and press for a decisive result. Carthage still had a substantial navy, although it may not have been as well trained as it had been before 265, but it had lost its bases in Sicily, Sardinia and the lesser islands of the Mediterranean as a result of the earlier defeat. Oared warships carried an exceptionally large crew in proportion to their size and had little space for provisions. As a result their operational range was small and without the island bases it was impractical for Hannibal to launch and support an invasion of Italy by sea. In addition Rome possessed a powerful navy which may have prevented a landing in the first place. Hannibal therefore adopted the logical alternative of reaching Italy by marching overland from his base in Spain. It was an exceptionally imaginative and highly bold plan. It required the army to force its way over great distances, past considerable geographical obstacles, and perhaps overcome the resistance of hostile peoples, before it was even in a position to strike at the real enemy. Only then could Hannibal begin the task of smashing Rome's armies, capturing her towns and cities, ravaging her fields, and subverting her allies. The Roman Republic had managed to endure huge losses during the First Punic War and still continue fighting, but then the disasters had always occurred at a distance. Now Hannibal planned to inflict as great, if not heavier, defeats in Italy itself.

Hannibal's plan was bold and more characteristic of Roman than Carthaginian military doctrine. Even the most pro-Roman of our sources recognized his ability as a general, but also tended to depict him as devious and treacherous, traits they considered to be characteristically Punic. Others, including Polybius, repeated the accusations that Hannibal was excessively avaricious and inhumanly cruel. The first charge may in part have reflected his never-ending need for money to fund his campaign and pay his soldiers. Polybius also suggested that some of the more brutal acts attributed to the general were in fact the work of his namesake, Hannibal Monomachus (the duellist), a vicious individual who was supposed to have suggested accustoming the soldiers to eat human flesh to ease the problems of supplying the army. The character of Hannibal remains surrounded by so much propaganda and myth that it is impossible to separate fact from fiction and say much about the real man.[7]

INVASION, 218–217 BC

The march to Italy was an epic in itself, but its details need not concern us here. When in November 218 the tired and weary survivors of the army came down from the Alps somewhere near modern Turin, there were only 6,000 cavalry and 20,000 infantry left. Though few in number, these were the pick of the army, veterans of years of hard fighting in Spain, who were confident in themselves and their leaders. In time their numbers would be swollen by Gallic warriors from the area, whose tribes had already risen in rebellion against the Romans trying to colonize their territory.

The Roman Senate had not dreamed that the Carthaginians would attempt anything so rash as the invasion of Italy. Two senior magistrates, the consuls, were elected each year to provide both civil and military leadership for the State, and where these men were sent always indicated the Senate's priorities. In 218 one consul, Titus Sempronius Longus, was sent to Sicily to prepare an invasion of Africa, whilst the other, Publius Cornelius Scipio, was to take an army to Spain and confront Hannibal. In this way the Romans intended to attack Carthage itself and the Punic general who had started the war, putting maximum pressure on the enemy in an effort to force a decisive result. The Senate does not appear to have anticipated that the Carthaginians would do anything other than defend themselves. Ancient states and armies possessed very limited long distance intelligence and it was some time before the Romans found out what Hannibal was doing. Scipio's expedition to Spain was delayed when some of his forces were diverted to face the Gallic rebels in the Po valley and others had to be recruited to replace them. When he finally began to ship his army to its destination, he stopped at Massilia (modern Marseilles), the Greek colony in Southern Gaul which was one of Rome's oldest allies, to gather supplies and intelligence. The consul was shocked to discover that Hannibal's army was no longer in Spain, but at that moment crossing the River Rhône. A cavalry force sent out to reconnoitre bumped into a similar detachment of Numidian light cavalry from the Punic army and beat them in a brutal skirmish, but failed to discover much information about the enemy. Scipio disembarked his army and marched to confront Hannibal, only to find that

Next page:
Hannibal's march to Italy was one of the great epics of the ancient worlds, rivalling the journeys and labours of Hercules, to whom the Carthaginian was sometimes compared. Even before he could begin his campaign against Rome, he had to defeat tribes in Spain and Gaul, as well as crossing physical obstacles such as rivers and mountains. His losses were heavy, but the best and most experienced soldiers completed the journey and proved a formidable fighting force. Some details of his route, and in particular the pass he took across the Alps, remain subjects of fierce dispute.

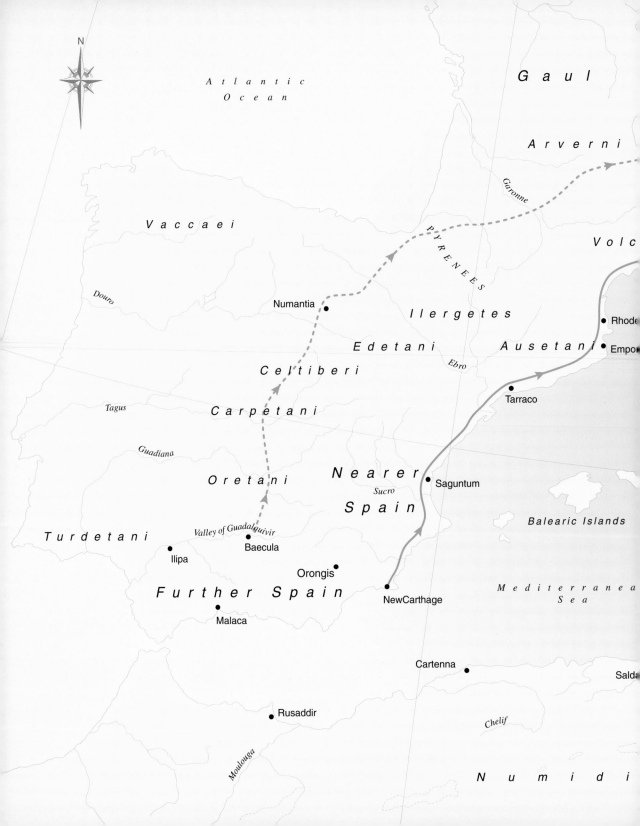

Hannibal's March to Italy and the campaign in the Po Valley

- - → Hasdrubal's probable route
—→ Hannibal's route
░ Roman territory
)(Alpine Passes

0 100 200 Miles
0 100 200 Km

...broges
Salassi
S
P
Insubres
Cenomani
Ticinus ✕
Placentia
Boii
v a r e s
T a u r i n i
Trebia ✕
...ausio
Genoa
Bononia
Ariminum
Fanum Fortunae
Massilia
Pisae
Arretium
Lake Trasimene ✕
Perusia
Asculum
Corsica
A d r i a t i c   S e a
Rome
Gerunium
Ostia
Salapia
Allifae
Cannae ✕
Capua
Beneventum
Canusium
Brundisium
Sardinia
Nola
Venusia
Neapolis
Heraclea
Tarentum
T y r r h e n i a n   S e a
Croton
Locri
Drepana
Messina
Rhegium
Lilybaeum
Sicily
Syracuse
Carthage
Aspis
Camarina
Neapolis
Hadrumetum
Theveste
M e d i t e r r a n e a n   S e a

The Battle of Trebia was fought on this plain within a day or two of the winter solstice in 218. A Roman army half the size of the one which would fight at Cannae was destroyed here.

he had moved on some days before, which was probably just as well, as the Romans were significantly outnumbered. He returned to the fleet, sent a report to the Senate and, after dispatching the bulk of his forces to Spain under the command of his elder brother Cnaeus, returned to Italy to take command of the troops already fighting the Gauls in the Po valley.

The news of Hannibal's march towards Italy stunned the Senate, and immediately prompted a change in the Roman plans. Sempronius Longus was recalled from Sicily and instructed to join forces with Scipio in Cisalpine Gaul to confront the invader. It took time to carry out this move and before this Hannibal arrived. Scipio behaved as aggressively as he had on the Rhône and immediately moved to fight the enemy in battle, but he was defeated in a cavalry engagement near the River Ticinus. Scipio's Roman, Italian and Gallic cavalry were outnumbered and enveloped by the Punic horse. As his troops fled the consul was badly wounded, and only escaped capture when his teenage son, also called Publius, led a body of horsemen to his rescue. The Roman army retreated in some disorder, destroying the bridge across the Ticinus and moving back to a position outside the Roman colony of Placentia (modern Piacenza). In December Scipio was joined by Sempronius Longus, who soon afterwards won an action which had escalated from a minor skirmish. Polybius praised Hannibal for accepting this minor defeat instead of feeding more and more troops into the fighting and allowing a battle to develop which was not under his control. Our sources now claim that there was a dispute between the two consuls, Scipio arguing for avoiding battle until the Roman soldiers had received more training, and Longus for an immediate battle. This caution seems out of character with Scipio's earlier boldness on the Rhône and before Ticinus. Perhaps his wound had depressed him, but it is more probable that his alleged opposition to fight a battle was intended by Polybius to exonerate him from blame for the subsequent defeat.

Sometime near the winter solstice, Sempronius was lured into fighting a battle on the open plain west of the River Trebia. Hannibal's army had grown to 10,000 cavalry and 28,000 infantry, and thirty or so elephants. The Romans mustered around 36,000-38,000 infantry, but only 4,000 cavalry, many of them demoralized by their recent defeat at the Ticinus. Hannibal had chosen the ground carefully, concealing 2,000 men in a drainage ditch behind the Roman line. The Carthaginian cavalry was divided equally between the two wings, outnumbering their Roman counterparts by more than two to one. The flanks of his infantry line were reinforced by the elephants. In the ensuing battle the legions managed to punch through Hannibal's centre, but first the Roman cavalry wings and then the flanks of their infantry were overwhelmed and collapsed. The 10,000 Romans who had led the attack in the centre were able to escape in good order, for Hannibal had no reserves to send against them, but the rest were captured, killed or scattered. This first great Carthaginian victory was a major shock to the Romans. Even more importantly it gave momentum to Hannibal's campaigns and practical support as more and more Gauls joined his army or brought it supplies.

**The Battle of Trebia,
December 218 BC**

Carthaginians

Romans

Placentia

Trebia

Camprenoldo
di sopra

Casaliggio

Costa

Camp of
Hanibal

Tuna

Trebia

Settima

Molinazzo

Canneto

Gazzola

Gandore

Riazzolo

Gerosa

Colomba

Rivalta Trebbia

Podenz

Niviano

Grazzano

Trebia

Ancarano

Camp of
Sempronius

Pieve
Dugliara

Camp of
Scipio

0   2   Miles

0   2   Km

N

The remaining months of winter, when the weather was poor and it was virtually impossible for armies to feed men and horses in the field, saw the usual period of inactivity as both sides prepared for the spring campaign. It was clear to the Senate that Hannibal's army must go one of two ways, since it could not ignore the great barrier formed by the Apennines. Therefore the two new consuls were positioned with their armies on either side of these mountains. Cnaeus Servilius Geminus was stationed at Ariminum (modern Rimini) in case Hannibal thrust down along the coastal plain of Eastern Italy, whilst Gaius Flaminius' force lay to the west of the mountains at Arretium in Etruria. Neither of the consuls was really strong enough to face Hannibal on his own, and it was intended that the two armies would join forces as soon as it was clear which direction the enemy had taken. In the event Hannibal moved faster than the Romans expected and took an unorthodox route. He crossed the Apennines quickly, and then forced his army through the difficult marshy country around the River Arno. Before Flaminius was aware of his presence, Hannibal was past Arretium and heading south. The consul sent word to his colleague and led his army in pursuit.

Flaminius was a 'new man' (*novus homo*), the first in his family to hold Rome's highest magistracy, which was usually dominated by a small group of aristocratic families. His career had been distinguished, for he had already been consul once before in 223, when he won a victory over the Gauls of the Po valley. It had also been highly unorthodox, and had won him many enemies, all ready to savage his reputation after his death. His disrespect for convention and proper ceremony was demonstrated by his decision to begin his year of office in 217 not at Rome, where consuls normally performed a series of religious rites, but actually with the army. Later he was depicted as dangerously rash, but the enthusiasm and confidence with which he pursued

The Battle of Trebia was fought in December 218 and was the first time Hannibal faced a full Roman army in battle. The battle was fought on ground of his own choosing, and he was able to conceal 2,000 men commanded by his brother Mago in a drainage ditch behind the Roman lines. Having a significant numerical advantage in cavalry, he further strengthened his wings with war elephants. Although the Romans were able to break through his centre and escape, their flanks collapsed and the bulk of the army was destroyed.

Hannibal's army was no less bold than that displayed by first Scipio and then Sempronius Longus in the previous campaign. Flaminius shared the anger of his men as they passed devastated villages and farms, burnt by Punic soldiers. Such devastation was normal in the wake of an invading army, but Hannibal had ordered his men to be especially brutal and thorough in their depredations. Rome and its allies were still fundamentally agrarian societies and the laying waste of their farmland was a serious blow, especially since an enemy's freedom to cause such havoc suggested their own military weakness. Flaminius urged his army on to pursue ever more closely, telling his men that the enemy's reluctance to face them was the result of fear.

On the shores of Lake Trasimene, the route ran through a narrow plain between the shore and a line of hills. Hannibal's army marched along this with the Romans just within sight, but in the night it doubled back to take up ambush positions parallel to the road. The next day, 21 June 217 BC, the Roman army left camp at dawn to follow the enemy. Thick mist, common in the area at this time of year, added to the confusion as the Roman column was suddenly attacked in the flanks and rear, which prevented the creation of anything like an organized fighting line. The Romans fought hard, resisting for three hours, but the issue was never in doubt. In the end they were killed, captured or drowned as they tried to swim to safety across the lake. Flaminius was cut down by a Insubrian horseman, a representative of one of the tribes he had defeated in 223. Only the vanguard, some 6,000 men, failed to encounter serious opposition and escaped from the trap, but even these were subsequently rounded up by the victorious Carthaginians. Flaminius' army of 25,000–30,000 men had been effectively destroyed, but the cost of 1,500–2,500 Punic casualties testified to the struggle that some had managed to put up. The other consul, Geminus, was hastening to join Flaminius and had sent his cavalry on ahead. This force, nearly 4,000 men commanded by Gaius Centenius, was ambushed and killed or captured by the enemy before they learned of the disaster. Without its mounted arm, the second Roman army was for the moment crippled.

'THE DELAYER', SUMMER TO AUTUMN 217 BC

The fundamental principle of Roman government was that no one individual should hold supreme power and that all power should be of a limited duration, normally a year of office. This was intended to prevent the emergence of a tyrant or king. Therefore there were two consuls in each year, whose power was absolutely equal. Only rarely was this principle abandoned for a short time and the rare expedient taken of appointing a dictator with supreme authority to direct the state. The dictator held office for six months and had not a colleague but a junior assistant, known as the Master of Horse (*Magister Equitum*). When the office of dictator had been created in the archaic period, it was considered important that he should fight with the infantry of the phalanx, the yeoman farmers who were the heart of Rome's military power, and so he was prohibited from riding a horse, leaving his deputy to command the cavalry. Such a restriction was no longer appropriate for the task of commanding the much larger and more sophisticated armies of the late third century BC, and one of the first actions of the newly appointed dictator, Quintus Fabius Maximus, was to gain special permission from the Senate to ride a horse.

Fabius was now 58, rather old for a Roman general, and had served as a youth in the First Punic War, subsequently being twice elected to the consulship. Aided by his Master of Horse, Marcus Minucius Rufus, himself a former consul, the dictator threw himself into reorganizing Rome's defences. Soldiers were enrolled and organized into new units and, once he had taken over Servilius Geminus' army, Fabius had an army of four legions, perhaps 40,000 men, at his disposal. It was weak in cavalry and contained a mixture of recent recruits with little training and more experienced men still dismayed by the recent defeats, but the creation of such a large field army in such a short time was an impressive achievement. Flaminius' defeat was blamed upon his failure to observe the proper religious rites and Fabius ordered that these now be most scrupulously performed.

Hannibal had moved east after Trasimene, crossing the Apennines again and marching into the coastal plain of Picenum, where he rested the army, for its health had still not fully recovered from the exertions of the last twelve months. For the first time since leaving Spain, Hannibal was able to send a message to Carthage reporting his achievements and requesting support. He remained highly confident and, when Fabius advanced and camped nearby, the Carthaginian immediately deployed his army to offer battle. Fabius declined, keeping his army on the high ground just outside the rampart of his camp and in such a strong position that Hannibal did not want to risk attacking. Battles in this period, apart from such rare ambushes as Trasimene, usually occurred by mutual consent, and even the most gifted commanders could rarely force an unwilling enemy to fight. Hannibal told his men that the Romans were frightened of them and moved on, devastating the countryside as he did so. This might provoke Fabius to risk a battle and if not it would demonstrate that Rome was militarily weak and unable to protect its own or its allies' fields. From the beginning of the Italian invasion, Hannibal had made great efforts to persuade Rome's allies to defect, treating allied prisoners very well and continually assuring them of his good intentions. As yet, apart from a few individuals and the Gallic tribes of the North, this policy had not borne fruit.

Fabius continued to avoid battle, but shadowed the enemy, sticking to the high ground and always adopting very strong positions. The Romans tried to ambush Hannibal's raiding and foraging parties, inflicting some loss, but could not prevent the enemy from moving at will. Hannibal made another of his sudden, unexpected moves, swooping down into the *ager Falernus*, the rich plain of Campania. Fabius countered by occupying a hill overlooking the pass, which Hannibal was most likely to cross once he had finished plundering. Hannibal tricked him again, drawing off the garrison actually guarding the pass by driving a mass of cattle up the path. It was night, and with flaming torches tied to their horns the animals looked like a marching column. In the confusion, the main army escaped without loss, and even wiped out the small Roman garrison, whilst Fabius' army remained in camp and did nothing. From the beginning the dictator's strategy of avoiding battle was unpopular with the army and the population in general. He was nicknamed 'Hannibal's *paedogogus*' after the slave who followed a Roman schoolboy carrying his books. The humiliation of watching as an enemy devastated the Italian countryside was deeply felt. Most Romans of all social classes continued to believe that bold action was the proper way to fight, desiring open battle, where Roman courage would prove victorious as it had so often in the past. Fabius' unpopularity grew, and in an utterly unprecedented move, Minucius was voted equal power with the dictator. The Master of Horse took over half the army, but was soon lured into battle by Hannibal, ambushed and badly mauled. Another disaster was only prevented by the arrival of Fabius' men, who covered the retreat. Minucius voluntarily returned to his subordinate rank and the remainder of the campaign was conducted under Fabius' command and according to his policy of avoiding battle. In the late autumn the dictator's six months' term of office expired and he and Minucius returned to Rome. The army, which was by now observing Hannibal's winter quarters at Gerunium, was left under the command of Servilius Geminus and Marcus Atilius Regulus, the consul elected to replace Flaminius.[8]

Soon after Fabius had assumed office he had issued a general order to the rural population in the regions threatened by Hannibal, instructing them to seek shelter in the nearest walled town, taking with them their livestock and all the food that they were able to carry, and destroying what was left. The aim, as with his continued harassment of Hannibal's foraging parties, was to deprive the Punic army of supplies. After Cannae, and especially in Livy's narrative, it was claimed that Fabius had understood the secret of defeating the enemy. Hannibal should not be faced in battle, but slowly starved into submission. Without food, his motley collection of mercenaries would desert or flee and the invasion would fail. This is clearly a great exaggeration, and even in Livy's own narrative Fabius' strategy appears to have inflicted little real loss on the enemy, and certainly never prevented Hannibal from moving wherever he wished. Fabius Maximus realized that after Trasimene the Roman army was not in a fit state to engage in an open battle with any chance of success. Therefore he avoided battle, and struck at the enemy in the only ways possible, skirmishing with small detachments and making it as difficult as possible to gain supplies. This is very much in accordance with the Hellenistic military wisdom of the era, when a general should only seek battle when he had a reasonable hope of success; if he had not, then he should avoid contact, but seek to build up his own strength and reduce the enemy's until winning a battle was more practical. The instinctive reaction of most Roman commanders was to seek direct confrontation as soon as possible. Fabius realized that this was unwise at that time, but still had trouble restraining his subordinates. The nickname he subsequently earned, 'the Delayer' (*cunctator*), paid tribute to his will power.[9]

THE ROMAN MILITARY SYSTEM

Rome did not employ professional soldiers. Instead, uniquely amongst powerful states by this period, she continued to rely on temporary militias, raised whenever required and then disbanded at the end of a conflict. Every five years a census was carried out of all Roman citizens, listing their property. Soldiers were expected to provide their own weapons and equipment, therefore a man's census rating determined not only whether or not he was eligible to serve, but also in what capacity. The majority of Roman soldiers owned small farms, since land was the main basis of wealth. As citizens they were legally obliged to serve for up to sixteen years or campaigns, but until the Punic Wars such prolonged military service was extremely unusual.[1]

The word legion (*legio*) had originally meant levy and referred to all the troops raised by the Republic in one year, but by this period the legion was the basic building block of the Roman army. Our best description of the legion is provided by Polybius and was written in the middle of the second century BC, more than sixty years after Cannae. The historian claims that his description does in fact refer to the war with Hannibal, and his narrative of these campaigns was certainly based upon this assumption. However, it has sometimes been suggested that the army did not assume this form until after Cannae and that at the time of the battle its structure was much less flexible. There is insufficient evidence to solve this question with absolute certainty, but the evidence for a major reform of the Roman army after Cannae is unconvincing, and rests largely on a single passage of Livy describing a local tactical ploy used in 211.[2] On the whole it is likely that the Roman military system in 216 BC differed only in minor details from Polybius' description.

This bronze Boeotian helmet was found in the River Tigris, but is an example of a type commonly worn by Roman cavalrymen. These helmets were made from sheet bronze which was hammered over a carved stone to give it its distinctive shape.

The Polybian legion consisted of cavalry, heavy infantry, and loose order skirmishers. Cavalry were provided by the wealthy equestrian order and included the sons of many senators, eager to make a name for courage and so help their future political careers. Their equipment had been copied from the Greeks and consisted of bronze helmet, mail armour or a metal or linen cuirass, circular shield, sword, spear and javelins. Later Roman horsemen employed the four-horned saddle, which provided an excellent seat, and it is distinctly possible that this was already in use. The basic organization was the *turma* of thirty, subdivided into three groups of ten each led by a decurion. Normally there were ten *turmae* per legion, providing a cavalry force of 300, but we also read of legions with only 200 cavalry, so this probably varied.[3]

The main strength of the legion was its heavy infantry, who were divided into three lines on the basis of age and experience, since all possessed the same property qualification. The first line (*hastati*) consisted of young men in their late teens or early twenties, the second line (*principes*) were men in their prime

Antenna type sword, the most common sidearm of the Spanish infantry at Cannae.

(which for the Romans was considered to be the late twenties), whilst the third line (*triarii*) was composed of the experienced, older men. Each line was divided into ten basic tactical units, the maniples, but for administrative purposes these were split into two centuries each commanded by a centurion. The centurion of the right-hand century was senior to his colleague, and commanded the whole maniple when both officers were present. Centurions were appointed or elected from amongst the ordinary soldiers. Each was assisted by his second in command (*optio*), a standard bearer (*signifer*), trumpeter (*cornicen*), and a guard commander (*tesserarius*).[4]

The soldiers in all three lines carried the same defensive equipment of a bronze helmet, a pectoral or chest plate, probably a greave for the left leg, and a bodyshield (*scutum*). This was oval in shape, about 1.2m (4 feet) in length and 60cm (2 feet) in width and constructed from three layers of plywood, each laid at right angles to the next. It was thicker in the centre and flexible at the edges, making it very resilient to blows, and the top and bottom edges were reinforced with a bronze edging to prevent splitting. Good protection came at a price, for the Roman shield was very heavy, around 10kg (22 pounds), and in battle its entire weight was borne by the left arm as the soldier held the horizontal handgrip behind the boss. Wealthier soldiers replaced the bronze or iron pectoral with a cuirass of mail or scale armour which, although heavier, offered far better protection. All soldiers carried a short thrusting sword, which probably was already of the type known as the Spanish sword (*gladius hispaniensis*) – the classic sidearm of the Roman soldier for over five centuries. Most also carried a dagger. The *triarii* were armed with thrusting spears, up to 2m. (8-9 feet) in length, but the *hastati* and *principes* both carried the famous Roman *pilum*. This was a heavy javelin consisting of a wooden shaft some 1.2m (4 feet) in length attached to a narrow iron shank 60cm (2 feet) long, topped by a small pyramid-shaped point. All of the weapon's weight was concentrated behind the small tip, giving it great penetrative power. The length of the metal shank gave it the reach to punch through an enemy's shield and still go on to wound his body, but even if it failed to do so and merely stuck in the shield it was very difficult to pull free and might force the man to discard his weighed-down shield and fight unprotected. The *pilum's* maximum range was about 29m. (*c.* 100 feet), but its effective range something like half that. According to Polybius each soldier carried two *pila*, one lighter than the other, but the archaeological evidence suggests rather more variety than such a simple, clear division.[5]

Supporting the heavy infantry and cavalry were the light infantry skirmishers or *velites*, recruited from the poorer citizens and those as yet too young to serve in the *hastati*. They were armed with a small round shield, sometimes a helmet, a sword, and a bundle of javelins, but it is unclear whether they were organized into units and how they were commanded. Many wore pieces of animal skin, especially wolf skin, attached to their helmets and Polybius believed that this was intended to allow senior officers to recognize individuals and reward or punish their behaviour, but is vague as to who these officers were. The number of *triarii* was fixed at 600 in ten maniples of sixty, but the remaining infantry strength of the legion was divided equally between the *hastati, principes* and *velites*. A legion normally had 4,200 foot, and therefore there were 1,200 men in each of these contingents, but in times of particular crisis the total might be increased to 5,000 or even more. As a result, the size of a maniple of *hastati* or *principes* could vary from 120 to 160 men when the legion was first formed and before any campaign losses had occurred.[6]

In battle the three lines of heavy infantry were formed one behind the other. In each line there was a gap equivalent to its frontage between each maniple. The maniples in the next line were stationed to cover the gaps in the line ahead, forming a *quincunx* pattern, like the 5 on a die. It has often been doubted that the legion actually fought in such an open formation, and various theories have been developed to explain how the intervals between maniples were closed just before contact, but such views are unconvincing and there is not a shred of evidence from our sources to support them. All armies formed battle lines with some intervals between their units, otherwise it was impossible to move without the units merging into one mass too large

for its officers to control, and the gaps in the Roman formation were wider than usual. The open formation gave the manipular legion great flexibility and allowed it to move across fairly broken country without losing order. With more than half of the legion in the second or third line, and thus uncommitted at the beginning of a battle, the Romans had plenty of fresh troops with which to plug a gap in their own line or exploit a break in the enemy's. Above the sixty centurions there were six military tribunes in command of each legion. A pair of these officers held supreme authority at any one time, but all were available to direct the legion in battle.[7]

Part of the relief on the first century BC altar of Domitius Ahenobarbus from Rome, this depicts soldiers wearing equipment very similar to that worn by the legions at Cannae. This scene shows a sacrifice of popanum cakes and a bull, part of the complex rituals required to prepare a Roman army for war. To the left of the altar stands an officer, most probably a military tribune.

The military tribunes, like all of the senior officers of the Roman army, were not professional soldiers but elected magistrates. The Romans did not maintain the strict division between army and politics common in modern democracies, and senators followed a career which brought them both military and civilian responsibilities, sometimes simultaneously. The two consuls elected each year were the senior magistrates and also provided the commanders for the most important of the State's wars. By modern standards they were amateurs, who received no formal training for command and instead learned by experience of service with the army in various junior capacities. The amount of military experience possessed by a consul inevitably varied considerably, but most displayed talent as leaders of men, even if they lacked the more technical skills of an army commander. Roman magistrates rarely stood for election on the basis of particular policies, instead relying on their reputation for ability. It was a system which heavily favoured a small group of wealthy aristocratic families who were skilled at promoting the virtues and successes of former generations and implying that as much or more could be expected from younger members of the family. With only two posts per year, competition for this high honour was intense, especially since a mixture of law and tradition prevented anyone attaining the rank before their early forties, and was supposed to prevent it being held twice within ten years. The vast majority of the 300 or so senators never became consul, and it was very rare even for the members of the established families to win the office more than once.[8]

The standard Roman army was commanded by a consul and consisted of two legions supported by soldiers from the Italian allies. The latter were organized into wings (*alae*) with roughly the same number of infantry as a legion, but as many as three times the cavalry. Each *ala* was commanded by three *praefecti* who were Romans, but very little is known about their internal organization and tactics. The *alae* were divided into cohorts, each provided by a single community, which appear to have varied in size from about 400 to about 600 men. It is unclear whether these were in turn subdivided into maniples, perhaps one for each of the three lines, or how often the cohort itself was used as a tactical unit. Our sources pay little attention to the allies, and give the impression that an *ala* operated in much the same way as a legion. The normal formation for a consular army was with the infantry of the two legions in the centre and an *ala* on either flank, so that the latter were usually known as the 'Left' or 'Right' *ala*. The cavalry of the two legions are usually depicted as stationed on the right wing, the place of honour, whilst the Latin and Italian horse formed on the left, but, given that there were often three times as many of the latter as the former, this may be an oversimplification.

The pick of the *alae* were drawn off to form the *extraordinarii*, élite cavalry and infantry at the immediate disposal of the consul, and sometimes these were used as a distinct tactical unit in battle. The entire consular army usually consisted of at least 20,000 men, but sometimes the military situation required a smaller force and a single legion and an *ala* might be employed. In this case the army was usually commanded by a praetor, the next senior magistrate, four of whom were elected in each year.[9]

The Roman army in this period functioned best at the level of the consular army and it was very rare for any enemy to pose so great a threat that the two consuls were required to join forces and give battle together. On the rare occasions that this was considered necessary, as when Hannibal invaded Italy, it was normal for the consuls to hold supreme command on alternate days. Deeply embedded in the Roman political system, and the military hierarchy was essentially an extension of this, was the desire to prevent any one man gaining overwhelming power. Therefore, just as in politics any grade of magistrate had several members, all with equal power, so also in the military organization there were three decurions to a *turma*, two centurions to a maniple, three prefects to an *ala* and six tribunes to a legion. Only with the appointment of a dictator was this principle abandoned for a set, six month period. Differences of opinion between consular colleagues Scipio and Sempronius Longus figure heavily in our sources before the defeat at Trebia in 218 and recur when Minucius Rufus was granted power equal to the dictator in the following year. It is clear that these narratives have been partially distorted by the desire of some senatorial families to absolve their members from blame for these defeats. However, this should not obscure the fact that the divided command was a weakness in the Roman military system when it was called upon to wage war at this level.[10]

Probably the greatest strength of the Roman military system was the vast reserves of manpower which underlay it. The precise figures may be questioned, but Polybius' survey of the male citizens and allies eligible for call-up in 225 BC produced a total of over 700,000. This gave Rome the capacity to absorb casualties which would have forced any other state to seek peace. It was especially difficult for the Hellenistic kingdoms to cope with heavy losses, both because of the time taken to train soldiers and also because of the relatively small population from which their recruits were drawn. In civilian life Roman citizens had considerable protection under the law, but nearly all of their rights were sacrificed as soon as they enlisted, legionaries willingly subjecting themselves to an extremely harsh system of discipline. The death penalty was inflicted even for such crimes as theft within the camp, and the punishments for flight, failure to perform duties, or for desertion were as harsh. The Roman army was highly organized and disciplined, and in these respects compared well with more professional forces. However, its essential impermanence was often a weakness. It took time to absorb recruits, train them to fight as units, accustom them to trusting each other and their officers. The longer a Roman army remained in existence, assuming that it did not suffer constant defeats, the more effective a fighting force it became. By the end of the Second Punic War some legions had been in constant service for over a decade and were as well drilled and confident as any professionals. Yet as soon as an army was discharged the whole process had to begin again. Each new levy usually included men with prior service, but they had not served together in the same legions and maniples under the same officers before, so still needed extensive training. Most Roman armies had the potential to be very efficient, but it took time and considerable effort on the part of its officers at all levels to realize this potential.[11]

THE CARTHAGINIAN MILITARY SYSTEM AND HANNIBAL'S ARMY

By the time of the Second Punic War Carthage had largely abandoned the use of citizen soldiers. The citizen population was too small to risk serious casualties and as a result Carthaginians were only required to serve in direct defence of their city, although in these rare cases their effectiveness proved low. Instead Punic armies relied almost exclusively on foreign soldiers. Some were genuine mercenaries, recruited as individuals or groups and serving purely for pay, but many more were soldiers provided by Carthage's subjects and allies, frequently led by their own chiefs or princes. Punic armies were therefore a heterogeneous mixture of races, and we hear of Libyans and Numidians from Africa, Iberians, Celtiberians and Lusitanians from Spain, wild tribesmen from the Balearic Islands, Gauls, Ligurians and Greeks. During the great mutinies at the end of the First Punic War, the rebellious soldiers had serious problems in communicating with each other. Normally the unifying bond was provided by the high command, all of whom were invariably Carthaginian. It is a tribute to these officers that the loyalty of the foreign soldiers serving Carthage was in general very good, the Mercenary War occurring in exceptional circumstances.[12]

Carthage maintained a much clearer divide between war and politics than Rome, and it was very rare for a serving magistrate ever to be given a military command. Punic generals were appointed and frequently served for many years with little interference or supervision of their actions from the civil authorities. As a result many were more experienced than their Roman counterparts, who were appointed annually. However, we should not exaggerate the difference, since Punic commanders were drawn from the ranks of the same aristocratic families who dominated politics. Military appointments appear to have owed more to wealth and influence than impartial assessment of military ability. Some Carthaginian generals were very able men, but, in spite of their longer commands, the majority did not prove themselves markedly superior to their Roman counterparts.

We do not have a detailed breakdown of Hannibal's army at the beginning of the expedition to Italy. The troops left behind in Spain or sent to Africa to guard against Roman attacks consisted of infantry and cavalry from at least five Spanish tribes, Balearic slingers, small numbers of Libyan cavalry and a considerable force of Libyan infantry, Liby-Phoenician (a people of mixed Punic and African stock who enjoyed limited rights) cavalry, Numidian horsemen from at least four tribes, and a small band of Ligurians from Northern Italy. The authority for the breakdown of these forces was a pillar

erected in Italy on Hannibal's orders, which makes it all the more frustrating that less information has been preserved about his own army. When he arrived in Italy, Hannibal had sizeable contingents of Libyan foot, Numidian horse, and Spanish cavalry and infantry, as well as a number of Balearic slingers, supported by war elephants (although all of the latter had perished before Cannae). He was soon joined by strong contingents from his new-found Gallic allies, who came to supply almost half of his field army. It is possible that Hannibal also had small contingents from some of the other ethnic groups, but if so their numbers were not great.[13]

The Libyan foot were the most reliable element in the army. Most fought in close order, although it seems likely that Libyans were also included amongst the *lonchophoroi*, Hannibal's specialist javelin skirmishers. (Many translations of Polybius render this inappropriately as 'pikemen'.) The heavy infantry began the war dressed in a version of the standard equipment of Hellenistic infantry. They wore bronze helmets and body armour, probably made from stiffened linen, carried large round shields and probably fought with spears. In 217 BC Hannibal re-equipped them with the spoils of the Roman dead at Trebia and Trasimene. It is not clear whether this means that he gave them only Roman defensive armour of helmet, mail cuirass, and oval *scutum*, or whether they also adopted the *pilum* and *gladius*. The Libyans were well disciplined and drilled, capable of complex manoeuvres, and in every respect the equals, and sometimes the superiors, of any Roman legionaries. If there were any Libyan or Liby-Phoenician cavalry with Hannibal's army, then they would have fought in close formation and carried Hellenistic-style equipment, not too dissimilar from Roman cavalry.[14]

The other African contingent was provided by the Numidians, most of whom fought as light cavalry. These men rode small, agile horses without saddle or bridle, wore a simple tunic and had only a small round shield for protection. Their tactics emphasized swift movement and avoidance of actual

This relief depicting an Iberian warrior, now in the National Archaeological Museum in Madrid, gives a good indication of the appearance of many of the Spanish troops at Cannae. He carries a flat, oval, shaped body-shield and wields a curved slashing sword or falcata. His headgear is curious in shape and may be some form of sinew cap.

contact, sweeping in to throw javelins and then retreating before the enemy could close. At the beginning of the war the Romans were unprepared for these tactics and had great difficulty coping with them. The Numidians were linked by language and culture but divided into fiercely independent tribes, themselves often wracked by civil wars as rival members of their royal families fought for power. However, the bond between Numidian royalty and Carthaginian aristocracy was often close; Hamilcar Barca was one of several Punic noblemen to form marriage alliances with princes from the various tribes. Such a means of cementing alliances was employed elsewhere by Punic noblemen, both Hasdrubal and Hannibal himself marrying Spanish princesses.[15]

The Spanish contingents provided close order cavalry, and both heavy and light infantry. The close order foot were known by the Romans as *scutati*, and carried a flat oval body shield. Some were also equipped with heavy javelin similar in size and effectiveness to the *pilum*. The skirmishers, or *caetrati*, carried a much smaller, round shield and a bundle of javelins. Foot and horse alike were also armed with high quality swords, either the short thrusting pattern copied by the Romans or the curved *falcata*, shaped rather like a Gurkha's kukri. The *falcata* is more prominent than the straight-bladed sword in the archaeological record, but this is most probably due to its use in ritual and sacrifice and it may in fact have been less common. The normal Spanish costume was a white or off-white tunic with a purple border, but there was probably considerable individual and regional variation. The slingers from the Balearic Islands were renowned for their skill and savagery in the ancient world. The combination of these men armed with longer ranged weapons and well trained and highly motivated javelinmen gave Hannibal a marked superiority over the Romans in light infantry actions.

The Gallic tribes provided Hannibal with both horse and foot. The cavalry fought in massed formation like the Spanish and were certainly using the four-horned saddle, which may in fact have been a Celtic invention. Helmets and

This statue from Vachères in Southern France could easily represent one of the wealthier warriors amongst Hannibal's Gallic allies. He wears a torc around his neck and has mail armour – a type which may well have been invented by the Gauls. He carries an oval shield and has a long sword at his belt.

especially armour were very rare amongst both Gallic and Spanish warriors, usually restricted to chieftains. For most warriors their sole defensive armour was provided by an oval or rectangular shield. The Gauls employed a variety of spears and javelins for throwing and/or hand-to-hand combat. Those Gauls rich enough to afford a sword tended to use a much longer, heavier weapon than the Spanish. Their blades might be 90cm (3 feet) or even more in length and frequently lacked a point. Instead the warriors relied upon the edge, slashing at their opponent and relying on strength more than finesse. We do not know whether some Gallic warriors fought as light infantry. Little prestige was associated with this type of fighting in tribal warfare and it seems to have been left to the poor or the young, but it is possible that some skirmishers were present with Hannibal's army.

We do not know the size of the basic tactical units in Carthaginian armies. It may be that the more regular elements, notably the Libyan foot, were formed into units of uniform size. However, it is probable that the other peoples provided war bands varying considerably in numbers. There are a few references to groups of 500 which may have been single units, and another to 2,000 Gauls divided into three bands, although in this case it is not clear whether these were in turn subdivided into smaller groups. Probably the basic units in the army consisted of a few hundred men, but some may have been as small as Roman maniples and others significantly larger.[16]

There really was no such thing as a typical Carthaginian army, since these varied tremendously in their ethnic composition, mixture of troop types and general effectiveness. Each general had to develop a system of controlling and co-ordinating the movements of the diverse elements within his army, a process which took time. Hannibal's army in the early years of the Italian expedition was the finest fighting force ever put into the field by the Carthaginian state. Its solid nucleus was provided by the men who had fought under Hamilcar, Hasdrubal and Hannibal's own command in Spain. These men were tough, experienced and highly disciplined. They knew and trusted their officers at all levels, and were personally loyal to the Barcid family who had given them victories and rich rewards in former campaigns. Most of the senior officers, who included Hannibal's younger brother Mago, were used to working under their young general and knew what he expected of them. The quality of Hannibal's senior subordinates was markedly higher than in the Roman army at Cannae.

Around this core of veterans, Hannibal was able to incorporate the Gallic warriors who joined him in Italy without any loss of the army's tactical flexibility. It took time for the Gallic contingent to become as reliable as the other troops, but this process of absorption had largely been completed by the date of Cannae. At Trebia the Gallic infantry were stationed in one sector of the line and appear to have fought under their own leaders just as if this were a tribal army. In the next year our sources noted the poor march discipline and low stamina of the Gauls, who were unused to such rigorous campaigning. By the time of Cannae small units of Gauls were interspersed with Spaniards, suggesting that the tribal structure had been substantially replaced by the same system of command which directed the rest of the army to perform the will of its Carthaginian officers. Still later, at the capture of Tarentum in 212, Hannibal made use of bands of Gauls specifically chosen for their speed and discipline, showing the extent to which these tribesmen had grown in efficiency during their long service. A similar process had probably occurred with most of the Spanish troops before 218; training, experience and discipline adding to the fierce bravery and individual skill at arms of these men drawn from warrior societies to produce highly effective soldiers.[17]

At Cannae Hannibal's soldiers formed a more united and cohesive force than their Roman opponents in spite of their much greater mix of languages and cultures. The Roman army in 216 was a very mixed bag, unused to working together and unfamiliar with many of its officers, a theme which we shall explore in more detail in the next chapter. Hannibal's army also possessed a much better balance between the different troop types. The Punic army had one cavalryman to every four infantrymen, compared to the Romans' ratio of one to thirteen. The Roman cavalry were significantly outnumbered and generally lacking in confidence. They also lacked the flexibility of Hannibal's men who included both light and heavy types. On a man to man basis the Carthaginian soldiers at Cannae were at least the equal of their Roman equivalents, and in the case of the cavalry and light infantry markedly superior. The real superiority of the Punic army came at higher levels, where its cohesion and efficient command structure gave it far greater flexibility in grand tactics and manoeuvre. The problem for the Romans in 216 was how to overcome this.

Fabius' dictatorship had given the Republic some respite after the disasters at Trebia and Lake Trasimene. A Roman field army had been rebuilt and had gained a little confidence through winning a few skirmishes with the enemy. The Romans had also enjoyed some success in Spain. Yet Hannibal, the man whose actions had provoked the conflict, was now spending his second winter in Italy at the head of an army undefeated in any serious engagement. Since 218 he had beaten two armies comprehensively, and destroyed or severely mauled several smaller forces, inflicting heavier losses than the Romans had suffered since the First Punic War. In many ways these disasters were worse, for they had occurred in the fields of Italy rather than on some distant sea and the losses had fallen heavily on the wealthier classes who served in the legions instead of the poor and politically less significant men who crewed Rome's fleets. The army, the source of Rome's military pride, had proved incapable of preventing an invader from marching where he willed, burning and despoiling the Italian countryside with impunity. This was a massive humiliation for any state, and a terrible admission of weakness. However well Roman forces did in Spain or Sicily, this was scant consolation for the continued presence of an undefeated Hannibal in Italy itself. Over the winter of 217–216 BC the Senate prepared to mobilize a large part of the Republic's resources to mount a massive war effort in the coming year. The other theatres, Spain, Sicily, and Cisalpine Gaul, were not ignored, but the main concern was always to be Hannibal.

This silver coin was minted in Spain by the Barcid family. On the reverse side is a war elephant. The face has sometimes been seen as the image of one of the Barcid family, perhaps even Hannibal himself, but is far more likely to be that of a deity.

THE LEADERS

In 218 and 217 the Senate had intended both consuls to join forces and defeat Hannibal, but Scipio had been wounded before Trebia and Flaminius killed and his army destroyed before Geminus' legions had reached them. This time the two new consuls would set out from Rome together, and the Republic's most senior magistrates hold joint command from the very beginning of the campaign. These men, Lucius Aemilius Paullus and Caius Terentius Varro, were elected to lead the largest army Rome had ever fielded to the anticipated great victory. In spring 216 it is doubtful that anyone could have guessed at the scale of the subsequent disaster, but all our sources were written with the benefit of hindsight. This makes it extremely difficult to separate myth and propaganda from truth, and so gain some genuine insight into the characters of these men.

Aemilius Paullus was the grandfather of Scipio Aemilianus, Polybius' patron, and as a result receives very favourable treatment from the Greek historian. In Polybius' account it was he who made the greatest efforts in organizing and encouraging the newly raised legions. Varro is mentioned as Paullus' colleague, but then does not appear again until the consuls have led the army to within sight of Hannibal. At this point a dispute broke out between the two Roman commanders over what to do next, Paullus advocating a far more sensible course than the less experienced Varro. It is only really at this stage and in the ensuing battle that Polybius depicts Varro as an incompetent general. Paullus had already held the consulship in 219 BC, successfully campaigning in Illyria along with his colleague, Marcus Livius Salinator. This victory had been marred by scandal involving the distribution of booty, and although the chief blame had fallen on Salinator, Paullus had not emerged entirely unscathed. This seems to have made him especially eager to avoid criticism in his second consulship. The Illyrian War had involved combined operations between the fleet and army as the Romans operated along the Adriatic coast, but there had been no pitched battles. Command in such a conflict certainly made great demands on a general, but it should be noted that the skills required were not precisely the same as those needed to control a massive field army.[1]

In Livy's account, and the narratives of all later authors, Varro appears from the beginning as a dangerous fool. He had been quaestor in 222, was aedile in 221 and the praetor in 218, but is first mentioned by Livy as allegedly the only senator to support the bill granting Minucius equal power to the dictator in 217. Varro was a 'new man' (*novus homo*), one of that small number in any generation of Roman politics who were the first in their family to reach high office. Livy dismissively describes Varro's ancestry as 'not merely humble, but sordid'. He repeats, without saying whether or not he believed it, a claim that Varro's father was a butcher on a small scale, and that as a youth he worked in the business. This suggestion is rarely given any credence by modern historians, since it was typical of the vulgar abuse which was the common coin of political debate at Rome. The minimum property qualification required for membership of Rome's highest census rating, and thus the Senate, would also mean that, even if Varro's father had begun in business on a small scale, he had built up a considerable fortune by the time that the son inherited and embarked on a political career. The claim that Varro established a reputation in the courts by winning cases on behalf of dubious clients is again a fairly conventional accusation to level at a rival politician. Livy's Varro, like his Flaminius and Minucius, conforms to a theme running throughout his *History* which held rabble-rousing politicians responsible for most of the ills to befall the Republic, but even his own account of the election in 216 BC suggests that things were much more complicated than this.[2]

Livy says that when the first ballot was held only Varro was elected. He implies that the five unsuccessful candidates were far more distinguished and responsible, but it should be noted that none of these men ever seem to have gained high office, although it is possible that this was because some or all were killed during the war, perhaps even at Cannae. As a result of his success, Varro presided over a second election which chose Aemilius Paullus as his colleague. Normally the presiding magistrate could do much to influence the outcome of a ballot, but it is unclear to what extent Paullus could be considered Varro's choice as partner, since we are told that all the other candidates withdrew. It has been speculated that there was some connection between the two, even that Varro may have served under Paullus in Illyria, but this must remain conjectural. A 'new man' needed considerable political ability to win elections against rivals with famous names and many clients who would vote for them. It was rare for candidates to advocate specific policies, since the electorate was more concerned with the individual's virtues and character, but a 'new man' could not parade the achievements and quality of his ancestors and needed some other way of fixing his name in the public eye. Discontentment with Fabius Maximus' cautious leadership in 217 presented Varro with a popular cause which gave a boost to his election campaign. He may well have exaggerated his own aggressiveness and the perceived faults of the well established senatorial families as military leaders, and so by implication what could be expected from some of the rival candidates, for 'new men' tended to overemphasize their own attributes in an effort to compete. Latching onto a popular cause in this way was risky, but a *novus homo* often needed to take risks if he was to succeed. Finally, it is vital to remember that the voting system at Rome heavily favoured the wealthier classes. Varro's supporters came not primarily from the landless poor, a group always seen as foolish and fickle in our ancient sources, but from all levels of Roman society. To have achieved such overwhelming success in the first ballot, he must have had the support of many, perhaps even the majority, of the wealthy equestrian order and probably also the Senate. The desire to confront Hannibal, and thus to choose an aggressive commander who would do this, was widespread at all levels in Rome.[3]

There was until recently a tendency to understand Roman politics in terms of fairly clearly defined factions based around certain wealthy families who monopolized high office over successive generations. These groups were believed to have advocated consistent policies, so that for instance a relative of Fabius Maximus could be expected to favour avoiding battle with the Carthaginians and attempting to wear them down gradually. We know very little about most Roman magistrates apart from their names, and this interpretation appeared to allow us to understand more about changes in Roman policy and strategy since the name alone now suggested an individual's probable behaviour. Unfortunately, there is not a shred of evidence to support such a view and it has now been utterly discredited. Roman senators competed as individuals to gain office and the power, prestige and wealth which this brought. Families strove to win as much electoral success as possible for each new generation, not to further consistent policies in the Senate. Most of the 300 or so senators never held the consulship or praetorship, and the competition for these magistracies was always fierce, for there were inevitably far more candidates than there were posts. Equally importantly, the senatorial families formed a small social world and intermarried extensively. To interpret the elections for 216 as a victory for a Popular party, or, if a connection between Varro and Paullus is assumed, for the 'Aemilian and Scipionic' faction, is not supported by the evidence.[4]

Varro was clearly a shrewd politician, for otherwise as a *novus homo* it is unlikely that he would have reached the consulship, but it is difficult to say how capable he was as a soldier. Unlike Paullus, he had certainly never held a senior independent command, but then this was also true of most consuls in the third century BC. In the future Paullus' family continued to be far more influential than Varro's descendants and were able to shift the blame for Cannae onto the 'new man'. This view was carried over into the literary record by Polybius and followed by all subsequent authors. Whether or not Varro was as incompetent a commander as these narratives suggest is impossible to say, but it is hard to see much evidence of Paullus' greater experience and skill in the events of 216. Neither man was really prepared to control such a huge army, and both were utterly outclassed as a general by Hannibal, but this was also true of all other Roman commanders at this time. Wars in Illyria, or against Ligurian and Gallic tribes in Northern Italy who fielded armies of brave but ill-disciplined warriors, were poor preparation for facing an army as flexible and well led as Hannibal's. It was only after long years of war, during which senators saw far more active service with the army than had ever been the case before, that Rome started to produce officers who added the skills of generalship to the physical courage and leadership normally expected of a Roman aristocrat.

THE LED

Polybius tells us that in 216 BC the Senate decided for the first time in Rome's history to muster an army of eight legions, four for each consul. However, in his account of the Gallic invasion of 225 BC he also appears to say that the consuls were given four-legion armies, but this may be a misreading of the text from a statement that there were four legions in total, two for each consul. Another important difference was that in 225 the two consuls were not supposed to join forces and it was luck, rather than design, which brought both armies into contact with the Gauls at the battle of Telamon. In 216 BC both consuls with all eight legions were expected to fight together. Not only were there more legions than usual, but each unit was increased in size to 5,000 infantry and 300 cavalry. As usual, the number of Roman infantry was matched by the allies who also provided a higher proportion of cavalry.

This scene from Trajan's Column shows Roman legionaries harvesting grain, wearing the segmented armour of the Imperial Period. Maintaining an adequate supply of food was a continual problem for army commanders and a major factor in their decisions during the campaign before Cannae.

Polybius tells us that the army finally mustered 80,000 infantry and 6,000 cavalry, making it one of the largest forces ever put into the field by the Romans.[5]

Polybius' testimony is clear, but Livy says that the different sources for the battle included a huge variation in the size of the Roman army. He mentions the Polybian figure of eight legions of 5,000 foot and 300 horse, but according to another tradition, the army of four legions commanded by the consuls of 217 outside Gerunium was only augmented by a levy of 10,000 new recruits. If the latter account is true, then the army at Cannae may have been no larger than around 50,000 men. Several modern scholars have favoured this version, arguing that, since numbers were frequently exaggerated in ancient accounts or distorted as the manuscript was copied over the centuries, it is always better to accept the lowest figure. In this case at least, such a view is surely mistaken. Polybius is our earliest and most reliable source and his account is utterly consistent in assuming that there were eight legions. It would be very rash to reject such positive testimony from this source. Livy's narrative also assumed the higher estimate, when for instance he mentions that twenty-nine tribunes were killed in the battle and names six of the survivors. Since there were six tribunes per legion, this would indicate that at least six legions were present. Both sources also emphasize how great an effort the Romans made in this year in their determination to crush Hannibal. An army of 50,000 men would have given them no more than rough parity with the enemy and would not have been much bigger than the army soundly defeated at Trebia. The course of the campaign and battle certainly make far more sense if the full eight legions were present. It is possible that a reinforcement of about 10,000 men was needed to bring the army at Gerunium up to the strength, compensating for losses in the last campaign as well as the need to increase the size of each legion. In addition four complete legions plus allies were raised and sent from Rome to join the army. This reconstruction would accommodate both traditions, but must remain conjectural.[6]

The Roman legions in this period were not the long-lived institutions of the later professional army and appear to have been re-numbered each year. It is extremely rare for our sources to explain in detail when units were raised, disbanded, destroyed or incorporated into other units. The army at Gerunium consisted of the legions allocated to Servilius Geminus at the beginning of 217 and the units raised by the dictator, a total of four legions. Geminus' army was based around some of the survivors of Trebia, most probably Scipio's two legions, for Flaminius seems to have taken Sempronius Longus' men. These units had been badly mauled, first in the fighting with the Boii and Insubres, and then at the hands of Hannibal, so it is virtually certain that they had received strong drafts of replacements. In the aftermath of Trasimene most if not all of Geminus' cavalry had been killed or captured. Since then, all four legions had campaigned with Fabius Maximus and Minucius, winning some minor skirmishes, but also suffering some defeats. These were the best troops in the army. Many of their men were experienced, and, most importantly, that experience had been gained recently, alongside the same comrades and under the command of familiar officers. However, their service had not been dominated by successful fighting and it was only this, combined with good training and leadership, that was believed to raise an army to the peak of its efficiency.[7]

The four new legions were all recruited in late 217 or early 216. It took a good deal of time to organize each legion, dividing the recruits into their sub-units of century and maniple, decury and *turma*, and appointing officers to command them. It took even longer for them to train and drill, gradually developing trust in each other and their leaders to create a confident and effective unit. In spite of the earlier defeats it is clear that the Romans had not become daunted by their foe, but rather grimly determined to achieve victory. Livy says that this mood was reflected when the tribunes of each legion led the men in taking a formal oath 'Never to leave the ranks because of fear or to run away, but only to retrieve or grab a weapon, to kill an enemy or to rescue a comrade.' In the past he claims that this oath, the *sacramentum* which in a similar form would survive in the Roman army for centuries, had been taken voluntarily by the soldiers in their own centuries.[8]

Another indication of the mood of the times was the high number of senators and equestrians serving with the army. The Roman aristocracy earned the right to rule the Republic in peace through its willingness to provide leadership and risk its lives on the State's behalf in wartime. Between a quarter and a third of the Senate was present at Cannae, and most of the remaining senators had sons or other close relatives with the legions. Marcus Minucius Rufus, Fabius' *Magister Equitum* and a former consul, was one of many distinguished men serving as a military tribune or on the staff of one of the consuls. The tribunes of this year were, in general, far more experienced and capable than was usual. Of the six named tribunes who survived the battle, four went on to hold the consulship. It is also instructive to look at the four praetors elected for the year. Three, Marcus Claudius Marcellus (consul 222, praetor 224), Lucius Postumius Albinus (consul 234, 229, probably praetor in 233), and Publius Furius Philus (consul 223), were former consuls and the other, Marcus Pomponius Matho, had already held the praetorship in the previous year.

This scene from the altar of Domitius Ahenobarbus seems to show the enrolment of soldiers or perhaps the census of all citizens held every five years. The census listed each citizen's property and thus made clear the capacity in which he would serve when required for military service.

Marcellus and Albinus, both of whom were given field commands, in Sicily and Cisalpine Gaul respectively, were of the same generation as Fabius Maximus, men who had reached maturity during the First Punic War. The Romans were relying upon experience in the present crisis. It is another indication of Varro's widespread popularity that he achieved the consulship in a year when the magistrates were such a distinguished group.[9]

The field army in 216 was four times larger than a normal consular army and no one had experience of handling such a huge force. Tradition, created

on those very rare occasions when both consuls had fought together, dictated that command should be held by each consul on alternate days, emphasizing just how improvised the system for controlling this army would be. It is doubtful whether the four legions massing at Rome had much time to spare for training together and certain that there was no opportunity to integrate this force with the existing four-legion field army when the two were united. The Roman army in the Cannae campaign was large, and its officers and soldiers brave and enthusiastic, but there had simply not been the time to weld them into a coherent force. The army was capable of only the very simplest of manoeuvres or tactics, far less flexible and supple than Hannibal's veteran force. This difference was to have a fundamental influence on the forthcoming campaign.

The army sent against Hannibal was not the only one fielded by Rome in 216, although it was by far the largest. In all between fifteen and seventeen Roman legions were in service by the summer of 216, a total of perhaps 75,000–85,000 men, around a quarter of the number of citizens Polybius says were eligible for military service in 225. Supporting these were a similar number of allied soldiers.[10]

THE PLAN

The Romans mounted a massive military effort for 216, and it is worth considering their objectives. For Polybius the answer was clear: to seek battle with Hannibal's army and destroy it. This was the decision of the Senate, supported by both consuls and in keeping with the general mood of the population as a whole for swift, decisive action. The historian claims that Paullus made a speech to the army, explaining the mistakes which had caused the defeats at Trebia and Trasimene and assuring them that these would not be repeated. Convention encouraged an historian to invent speeches which he considered appropriate for the character and situation, so it unlikely that we have a quotation from anything which the consul actually said, but his favourable attitude towards Paullus does not prevent Polybius from depicting him as eager for battle. In this version, the dispute between the consuls is not over whether or not to fight Hannibal, but when and where to do so.[11]

From the very beginning Livy's narrative of the Cannae campaign is pervaded by a sense of approaching disaster, for which Varro is held almost solely responsible. He appears as a braggart, making speeches before he had even left Rome boasting of winning the war on the first day that he came in sight of Hannibal. Paullus is depicted as a friend of Fabius Maximus and an advocate of his delaying tactics. Both men were convinced of the futility of facing Hannibal's veterans in an open battle, preferring instead to harass the enemy and deprive them of supplies until starvation forced their flight or surrender. Fabius is given a long speech, arguing for caution and telling Paullus that he will have to contend as much with his consular colleague as with Hannibal. Livy's account of the campaign is, like so much of his work, intensely dramatic, as the wise Paullus manages to postpone, but cannot prevent the inevitable catastrophe brought on by Varro's rashness. The description of Paullus' death at Cannae, unwilling to survive a disaster for which he was not responsible even though its architect had already fled the field, is rich in pathos. This same tradition of consuls at loggerheads and of Paullus along with all 'wiser' senators supporting Fabius who continued to advocate caution was followed by all later sources.[12]

In 217, and later during his successive consulships in the remainder of the war, Fabius Maximus never fought a pitched battle with Hannibal. As dictator he had issued an order for villagers in the areas threatened by Hannibal to flee to the nearest walled town, taking with them livestock, moveable possessions and food. What could not be carried was to be hidden or destroyed. This 'scorched earth' tactic was intended to deprive the enemy of supplies, whilst the Roman army continually harassed and ambushed their foraging parties. In the end Hannibal's army must starve, for as yet no significant community or people in Central or Southern Italy had defected to his cause, and he was far too far away from the tribes of Cisalpine Gaul to draw supplies from them. Livy claimed that this strategy would have worked if only the Romans had continued it into 216, and that even in the weeks before Cannae the Carthaginian army was beginning to lose heart. Its Spanish contingents, tired of the poor rations and long overdue pay, were supposed to be planning to desert. Another rumour claimed that Hannibal had drawn up a plan to abandon the army and flee with all his cavalry, hoping to cut his way to Cisalpine Gaul. Plutarch has Fabius Maximus claim that if Hannibal did not win a battle within the next twelve months then he would be forced to retire. Thus Cannae became all the more tragic, and Varro an even bigger blunderer, for if only the Romans had followed the same cautious strategy in 216 then victory was within their grasp. It was only this stunning defeat which prompted a wave of defections so that nearly all of Southern Italy abandoned Rome, providing Hannibal with a secure base, and the resources of men and material, which allowed him to wage war in Italy for more than a decade.[13]

Polybius did not share this view. In his, and indeed to a great extent in Livy's, narrative, it is difficult to see much evidence for any real hardship being suffered by Hannibal's men. Supplying an army of around 50,000 soldiers, at least 10,000 cavalry horses, plus an unknown number of servants, wives and camp followers was a never-ending problem for the Carthaginian commander. Our sources frequently mention the activities of foraging parties and explain many of Hannibal's movements as dictated by the need to gather supplies. Fabius Maximus did very little to hinder these movements. The Carthaginians on several occasions took Roman strongholds, possessing themselves of the supplies massed at these points. Sufficient provisions were gathered at Gerunium to permit the Punic army to remain there for around six months from late autumn 217 to spring 216.[14]

Attacking an enemy army indirectly by depriving it of food was an approach sometimes adopted by later Roman armies, common enough to be known by the slang expression 'kicking the enemy in the stomach'. In 217 Fabius Maximus' main aim was to avoid further defeat whilst he rebuilt the army, and harassing the enemy was the only way to do this without risking fresh disasters. This was the right thing to do in the circumstances, but there is no reason to believe that this was still the right thing to do in 216, or even that Fabius himself believed this. The dictatorship had given Rome the chance to recover so that for the new campaign she was able to field a massive eight-legion army. Some of the troops were now experienced and well trained, and all were very confident. There was no reason to concentrate so many troops if an open battle was not

Hannibal's army remained almost constantly on the move during the campaigning seasons after his arrival in Italy. Once he had left Cisalpine Gaul early in 217 he was effectively cut off from any allies and could not rely upon them to supply his army. He moved with the intention of humiliating the Romans, by defeating their armies in battle or demonstrating their weakness, but he also had to bear in mind the need to supply his soldiers. His objective was to win over Rome's allies and weaken the Republic until it was willing to accept a negotiated peace.

Hannibal's progress through Italy

- ➔ Hasdrubal's probable route
- ➔ Hannibal's route
- ▢ Roman territory
-)(Alpine Passes

Taurasia

Cremona

Clastidium
Placentia

Padus

Genoa

Bononia

Ariminum

Colline Pass
Pistoria
Faesulae
Fanum Fortunae

Pisae

Arretium
Cortona
Lake Trasimene
Perusia

Asculum

Picenum

Spoletium

Umbria

Etruria

A P E N N I N E S

A P E N N I N E S

Paeligni

Corsica

Rome

Marsi

Samnium

Gerunium
Arpi

Salapia

Allifae

Cannae

Canusium

Ostia

Apulia

Caudini

Capua
Beneventum

Brundisium

Calabria

Neapolis

Tarentum

Lucania

Velia

Heraclea

Sardinia

*Tyrrhenian
Sea*

Adriatic   Sea

Cavales

Croton

Bruttium

Locri

Drepana

Messina
Rhegium

N

Lilybaeum

*Mediterranean
Sea*

Carthage
Aspis

Syracuse

Neapolis

Camarina

Hadrumetum

0   100   200 Miles

0   100   200 Km

planned, for half as many could have continued to shadow the enemy just as effectively. Supplying 80,000–90,000 men and their mounts created immense problems, making the army a very clumsy force to manoeuvre close to the enemy without actually fighting. Allowing Hannibal to maraud at will through Italy was a constant affront to Roman pride, a demonstration of the Republic's inability to protect itself and its allies. The appearance of power was often of more importance than its reality in the ancient world, and the continued perception of Rome's weakness would eventually encourage attacks upon her or rebellions amongst her allies. If Hannibal's army was seriously defeated in battle then it was too far away from its bases in Spain to survive. A single Roman victory would end the invasion and perhaps even the war. Seeking battle was the logical course of action for the Romans in 216, having amassed what they hoped would be overwhelming force. Perhaps Fabius Maximus still advocated caution – our sources certainly depict him as single-minded and unimaginative, although it was a tendency of ancient biographers to exaggerate aspects of a man's character – but it is unlikely that this view was either widely supported or correct.[15]

THE CAMPAIGN

As with so many other aspects of the Second Punic War, there is some doubt over the precise chronology of the Cannae campaign. The battle itself occurred on 2 August, and, as far as we can tell, the months in 216 were broadly in line with the modern calendar. Polybius tells us that Hannibal remained in his winter quarters at Gerunium until the year's crops had ripened sufficiently to be harvested and consumed by his soldiers. In this century that would place his move sometime in early June. If the third century BC and modern calendars were running reasonably closely, and assuming that the climate and hence the agricultural year were also essentially the same then as now, then this would mean that there were around seven to eight weeks of campaigning before the battle. Even a little variation in either of these factors could alter this by several weeks. Polybius tells us little about this period, his account only becoming detailed in the days immediately before the battle. Livy recounts a series of incidents, largely intended to demonstrate Varro's inexperience and rashness, but these make very little sense and appear to be inventions.[16]

When Hannibal left Gerunium he headed south into the fertile region of Apulia. He was followed at some distance by the Roman army which had observed the Carthaginians throughout the winter months. This remained under the command of Servilius Geminus and Atilius Regulus, the consul and suffect (replacement) consul for 217. A series of messages went back to Rome, reporting Hannibal's movements and asking for instructions. The two commanders explained that they could not remain too close to the enemy without being forced to fight a battle. The Senate's reply instructed them to wait until the new consuls arrived with their legions. Thus the Carthaginian army was virtually unmolested as it moved along the coastal plain and captured the hilltop town of Cannae, about 100km (60 miles) from Gerunium. Cannae was not the largest settlement in the region, nearby Canusium being significantly larger, and had probably suffered in the campaign of the previous year for it was now abandoned, although it was still being used as a supply dump by the Romans. A rich store of produce from the surrounding area fell into Punic hands, providing Hannibal with a most valuable bounty which reduced his need to move and forage for some time. The town's site also provided a good vantage point overlooking the flat plain to the north, the direction from which the Roman army would come.

We do not know how long it took the Carthaginians to move from Gerunium to Cannae, but once there Hannibal appears to have sat and waited for the Romans, perhaps for several weeks. There was no significant force to prevent him from moving wherever he liked in Southern Italy so the reason for this decision must be connected with his objective for the year's campaign. The Punic invasion of Italy was still precariously placed. Hannibal had won victories and suffered no significant reverse, but had failed to make allies apart from the Gallic tribes of the Po valley, with whom he had long since lost contact. So far all his blandishments to Rome's allies, and his kind treatment and release without ransom of allied soldiers taken prisoner, had not prompted the defection of any community. There was no reason to believe that a repeat of the previous year's foray across the Apennines would produce greater results. His battlefield victories and depredations had not as yet had a serious impact on the Romans, whose spirit was undiminished and resources scarcely dented. It is hard to know just how much, or how little, information was available to ancient generals when they made their plans. In his account of the winter, Livy mentions the arrest and mutilation of an alleged Carthaginian spy in Rome itself, claiming that the man had been there throughout the war. It seems probable that Hannibal had some idea of the large army the Romans had raised for this year, but it is impossible to be certain. If the Romans had decided to confront him in battle, then he could not be seen to avoid this threat, since no community would defect to an invader who lacked confidence in his ultimate victory. Hannibal's main objective was to meet and destroy the main Roman army or armies as he had in the last two years. Cannae, in open country well suited to his superior cavalry and where for the moment his men could live off the captured supplies and grain harvested from the fertile farmland nearby, offered an ideal spot to seek battle. The very willingness of the Punic army to wait there rather than camp in a strong position showed their confidence and acted as a challenge to Roman pride.[17]

Livy tells us that Paullus and Varro brought their forces to join the field army whilst it was still near Gerunium. On learning of this and of Varro's impulsive temperament, Hannibal attempted to lure the Romans into a trap by very visibly abandoning his camp, but concealing his army in ambush nearby. The whole story makes very little sense and is certainly to be rejected in favour of Polybius' version, which has the new consuls joining the army further south about a week before the battle. In one respect, however, Livy's account is certainly to be preferred, for Polybius claims that both Geminus and Regulus remained as proconsuls with the army and fell in the battle. Since Regulus survived to hold the censorship in 214, it is best to accept Livy's claim that he asked to be relieved because of age and returned to Rome before the battle.[18]

The new and old armies united, the two consuls led the combined force south. On the second day of their march they came within sight of Hannibal's army about 8km (five miles) away. The tread of so many men and animals in the Roman column must have thrown up an immense cloud of dust from the dry Apulian soil which would have made their approach visible from even further away. At some point during the next days, one of Hannibal's staff, a man named Gisgo, is supposed to have commented nervously on the size of the enemy host. Hannibal looked solemn and then quipped that even though there might be a lot of men over there, none were called Gisgo, dispelling the tension in laughter, though some of this may have been sycophantic. The route followed by the Romans is not altogether clear, but it may be that the new consuls had joined Servilius somewhere near Arpi. It is possible that they marched south along the coastal plain of Foggia for most of the way, and certain that the last stretch was across the open ground north of the River Aufidius. Cannae itself lay on a line of hills to the south of the river, but the ground to the north is very flat, with only the gentlest of gradients sloping down to the sea. The area then, as now, was highly cultivated and virtually treeless. Livy tells us that the Roman commanders took great care to reconnoitre the route they were following which suggests that some of the lessons of the last two campaigns had been learnt. Careful patrolling and the openness of the country ensured that any ambush was unlikely to succeed, so that Flaminius' mistake would not be repeated.[19]

Yet now that they were close to the enemy, Paullus is said to have been deeply unhappy about the ground and it is at this point in Polybius' narrative that the dispute between the consuls begins as they argued over where to fight the planned battle. Hannibal had more and better cavalry than the Romans, and Paullus believed that it was most unwise to fight him in open country so suited to mounted action. His preference was to move into more broken

Next page:
The Romans follow Hannibal to Cannae.
They most probably kept to the coastal plain, where the ground would not permit Hannibal to repeat the success of his ambush at Trasimene. As they came closer Hannibal sent out his cavalry and light troops to harass the advance. In spite of this, the Romans pushed on and camped north of the River Aufidius, later sending a detachment across to the other bank. Hannibal then moved his own base to face the main enemy camp.

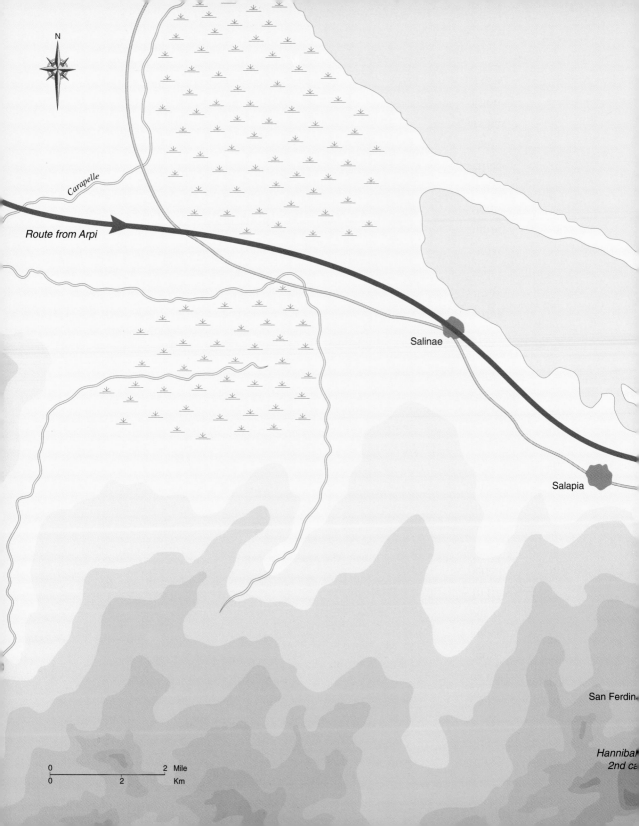

N

Carapelle

Route from Arpi

Salinae

Salapia

San Ferdin

Hanniba
2nd ca

0   2   Mile

0   2   Km

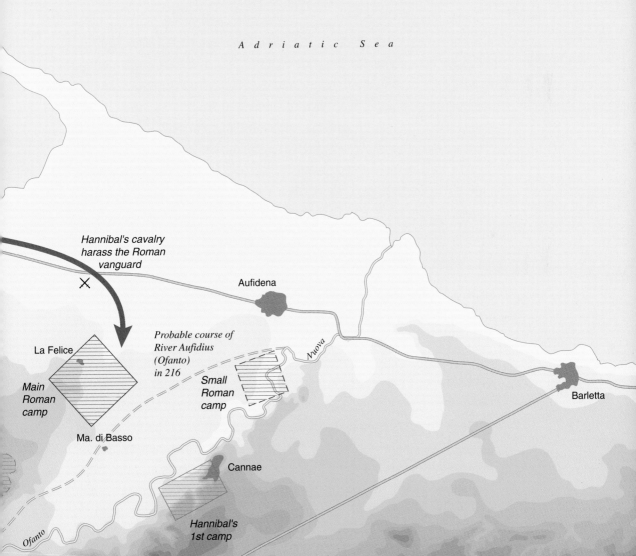

A d r i a t i c   S e a

Hannibal's cavalry
harass the Roman
vanguard

Aufidena

Nuova

*Probable course of
River Aufidius
(Ofanto)
in 216*

La Felice

**Main
Roman
camp**

**Small
Roman
camp**

Ma. di Basso

Cannae

Barletta

**Hannibal's
1st camp**

Ofanto

ground, probably in the hills to the west, and choose terrain where infantry rather than cavalry would be the decisive arm. Roman legions operated best on reasonably open ground, so it is likely that Paullus was most concerned with having some protection for the army's flanks. Varro appears to have disagreed and Polybius put this down to his inexperience, but it should be pointed out that Paullus' plan was not as simple as it seemed. In the first place the Roman army was exceptionally large and of very mixed experience, making it slow and clumsy. Such an army would have difficulty in out manoeuvring Hannibal's tightly controlled and cohesive forces and forcing him to fight on unfavourable ground. Feeding the Roman army was also a major problem, especially since the enemy now had possession of their most important supply dump in the area. Paullus' plan would mean keeping the entire army concentrated for a long time until its commanders had created an opportunity and it is highly questionable whether it would have been possible to supply it effectively.[20]

On the next day it was Varro's turn to command and he led the army nearer to the enemy in spite of his colleague's objections. Hannibal sent out cavalry and light infantry to harass the advancing Roman column. These caused some confusion, but when the Romans formed up some close order infantry, perhaps the *extraordinarii* – the picked allied troops who normally led the advance – and supported them with *velites*, the enemy were driven back. Sporadic fighting continued till nightfall, without either side winning a marked advantage or inflicting serious casualties, but the Romans' progress was dramatically slowed by the need to form and maintain a fighting line, and it is unlikely that the column had made more than a few kilometres by the end of the day. Paullus was still supposedly reluctant to fight in this terrain, but on the next morning he assumed command and led a further advance to camp close to the enemy. According to Polybius, the consul felt that he was now too close to disengage the army. Some modern scholars have doubted this claim and gone on to suggest that there was no real division of opinion between the consuls, but that is to misunderstand the difficulty of withdrawing in the face of the enemy. This was always a highly dangerous operation, especially so for a large and unwieldy army like the Roman army in 216, and one faced in open country by superior cavalry. To retreat without a fight from an enemy, especially an outnumbered enemy, was also deeply dispiriting. At present the Romans were enthusiastic and eager to fight, but such spirit could prove very brittle. On balance, Polybius was probably right to say that the Romans were by this time committed and could not really pull away without battle.[21]

It is possible that Paullus had misgivings, but the decision had already been made for him and he proceeded to make the best of the situation. He camped with the main force, about two thirds of the army, on the north bank. Hannibal still appears to have been positioned on the high ground around Cannae on the other side of the river. The remaining third of the Roman army was sent across to the southern or right bank of the Aufidius about a mile (1.6km) from the main camp, but somewhat further from the enemy. The willingness to send some troops across the river to the same side as the enemy demonstrated the Romans' determination and aggressive intentions. From this position they could more easily protect any foraging parties they sent to this side of the river, whilst threatening any of the enemy who attempted to do likewise. The dispositions of the Romans' camps were in themselves offensive acts, as they attempted to control as much of the surrounding area as possible. In practical terms this might cause the enemy supply problems, but more immediately it was part of the attempt to build up their own soldiers' confidence and diminish that of the enemy.

Apparently on the same day, Hannibal countered the Romans' aggressive moves by giving his men an encouraging speech and, more importantly, advancing to camp on the same side of the river as the Roman main camp. The most likely location for this is the long, flat topped ridge on which the modern town of San Ferdinando di Púglia now lies, for it is higher than the plain, giving it good defensive qualities, and close enough to the river to offer a convenient water supply. This was another statement of confidence, showing his willingness to close with and put pressure on the enemy, and his belief in victory. This careful, almost ritualized manoeuvring was typical of the formal battles of this period, each commander gradually building up the morale of his men giving them as many advantages as possible for the coming battle.[22]

The next day, 31 July by the modern calendar, the Carthaginian commander ordered his men to rest and prepare themselves for battle. Weapons and armour were cleaned, blades sharpened and as much effort as was practical on campaign taken to 'dress up' for a battle. On 1 August the Carthaginian army marched out and deployed in battle formation on the left bank of the river facing the Roman camp. It was once again Paullus' day of command and he refused to risk a battle. Covering forces were placed in front of each of the Roman camps, but they did not move far from the ramparts and nothing was done to provoke a battle. Hannibal kept his army deployed for several hours, but was largely content with the moral impression created by the enemy's refusal to fight, knowing that this would encourage his men. As was usual in these situations, he did not press the issue or attack the camps directly. The only move made was to dispatch the Numidian cavalry across the River Aufidius to threaten the smaller Roman camp. The light cavalrymen harassed the parties – probably mainly consisting of servants – out drawing water, panicking them and chasing them back into the camp itself. This was humiliating for the Romans, reminding them of the confidence the enemy had displayed earlier in the day by their offer to fight a battle in the open plain. It also challenged the very reason for the smaller camp's existence, which was supposedly to guard Roman foragers and threaten those of the enemy. Polybius and our other sources tell us that Varro and many of the Romans felt shamed by their failure to counter the Numidian raid. Perceptively, the Greek historian also suggests that the soldiers were chafing at the delay, knowing that a battle was coming and wishing to get it over with.[23]

Polybius claims that messages were received in Rome announcing that the consuls were facing Hannibal near Cannae and that skirmishes between the outposts were occurring regularly. The city was tense, but given the distance involved, it is unlikely that the news reached Rome much before the battle occurred, for on 2 August Varro decided to fight.[24]

Soon after dawn on 2 August the troops in the larger Roman camp formed columns in the main roads between the tent lines and in the open space (*intervallum*) behind the ramparts. Each maniple, legion and *ala* assumed a position in the column corresponding with its place in the battle-line. A camp normally had at least four gateways and each column marched out from a different gate. Varro led the army out of the camp and across the river. There was one ford between the two Roman camps, but there may have been other crossing places to the east which were also employed. On the right bank of the Aufidius, the army was joined by the troops from the smaller camp and together they deployed into battle order.

All our sources emphasize that the decision to deploy the army and offer battle was taken by Varro alone. This was right and proper, since it was his day to exercise command, but Livy goes so far as to claim that he issued the orders without consulting, or even informing, Paullus. In this version, Varro simply raised the red *vexillum* standard – the square flag which marked the commander's position during a battle – outside his tent, the traditional symbol to tell the soldiers to prepare for battle. He then formed his own legions into column and led them out. Paullus, seeing all this happen, felt obliged to follow with his own troops. None of this makes any sense. Varro held supreme command of the entire army for the day and it is absurd to suggest that he failed to issue orders to one important section of it or to inform his colleague. It should also be noted that the process of preparing the soldiers for battle and parading them preparatory to moving out was long and complex. Close supervision was required on the part of all the army's officers, and especially the military tribunes of the legions and *praefecti* of the *alae*, to ensure that this was carried out as smoothly and quickly as possible, checking that the columns used for deployment were formed in the correct order and that when the army finally was able to move out it went by the proper route to the right place. The process must have taken hours for any army, and was made especially difficult by the size and mixed levels of experience and drill of the soldiers at Cannae. It is impossible to imagine that Paullus was unaware of all the activity in camp until Varro had begun to lead his forces out.[1]

Aemilius Paullus cannot have been ignorant of his colleague's intention to offer battle on 2 August. The day before he had refused to meet Hannibal's challenge, keeping most of his soldiers inside the camps. This does appear to give a clear indication that Paullus genuinely believed that it was unwise to fight. Polybius claims that he felt supply problems would force Hannibal to move his camp within two days if there was not a battle. If the Carthaginian army was to disengage and withdraw, then this would encourage the Romans and perhaps grant them an advantage in any future encounter. The smaller Roman camp had been expressly set up to place pressure on the enemy's foragers. There was perhaps another reason why Paullus might have been less reluctant to fight a battle on the next day. As far as we can tell, on 1 August the Carthaginian army formed up between their own camp and the larger

Roman camp. Livy tells us explicitly, and Polybius appears to imply, that the Numidians had to cross the Aufidius in order to attack the smaller Roman camp which seems to confirm that the main Punic army had been formed up on the left bank of the river. Both of these sources make it clear that Varro led the troops from the larger Roman camp across the river to the same side as the smaller camp and deployed the combined army into battle order in front of it. He was not then accepting battle under precisely the same conditions that his colleague had declined the previous day. The Romans had deliberately chosen different ground, despite this involving moving the larger part of their forces to the new position. Varro could not even be sure that Hannibal would accept a battle in this new location, but may have felt that simply offering to fight would help to encourage his soldiers after the humiliation of declining battle and seeing one of their camps attacked. Perhaps Paullus still believed that it was unwise to fight, even in the alternative position. This is impossible to know, but it is worth remembering that the ability of the Numidians to dominate the eastern bank right up to the outposts immediately outside the smaller camp called into question the Romans' ability to deny Hannibal's army provisions.[2]

Whether or not Paullus agreed with his judgement, Varro had the right to make the decision and had not simply reversed his colleague's choice. Fighting on ground of your own choice was one of the skills of the good commander portrayed by Hellenistic military theory, and this was something which both Sempronius Longus at Trebia and Flaminius at Trasimene had failed to do. Before moving on to consider in detail the choice of battlefield and how the terrain affected the subsequent battle, it is worth mentioning a theory which claims that in fact Paullus rather than Varro was in command on 2 August and committed the army to battle. This is an attractive idea, allowing us to claim that we have seen through the propaganda in our sources, but is based on highly tenuous assumptions. It is much better to follow the literary tradition and accept that Varro was in command, although he may have acted with the approval of his fellow consul.[3]

LOCATING THE BATTLEFIELD

Panorama showing the view from Cannae today. The cluster of white buildings in the distance (centre) is San Ferdinando, the probable site of Hannibal's camp. The current line of the River Aufidius (Ofanto) is marked by the green line of low trees and bushes in the middle distance. The battle was fought on the level plain in the centre.

It is rare for the precise location of any battle fought in the classical world to be known with certainty. Literary style was important to ancient historians and too much topographic information was likely to overburden any narrative. As a result, even accounts written by senior officers who were present at a battle mention few geographical features. The campaigns in Italy from 218 to 216 BC are described in some detail by our sources and it is usually possible to determine the general area in which a battle occurred. It is then a question of attempting to relate the snippets of information provided in their accounts of the battle to the terrain in this area today in order to locate the battlefield. Most useful are those major geographical features which are unlikely to have changed in the last twenty-three centuries. Usually there are several sites in the right area which could conform to the ancient sources. The probable size of the opposing armies, their tactical systems and the objectives of each side in the campaign itself provide the context in which we must try to judge on which of these sites the battle is most likely to have occurred. This is an

uncertain process, inevitably relying on many guesses and impressions, and as a result it is unsurprising that there is a broad range of opinions concerning the site of most battles. Cannae is no exception to this.

The location of the town of Cannae itself on the line of hills south of the River Aufidius (Ofanto) is one of the few certainties, even if the Roman remains there in fact date to a later period. We know from our sources that the Roman army had constructed two camps. The larger camp lay on the side of the river from which the Roman army had approached Cannae and faced Hannibal's second encampment. The smaller camp was on the other side of the river, about a mile (1.6km) from the main position, and even further from the Punic camp. The battle was fought on the same side of the river as the smaller camp. Polybius tells us that the Roman line was formed with its right flank resting on the river and correspondingly that the Punic left was also anchored on the Aufidius. The Roman line faced south, the Carthaginians north, so that neither side suffered the disadvantage of fighting with the sun in their eyes. Other sources repeat a Roman tradition that their soldiers were

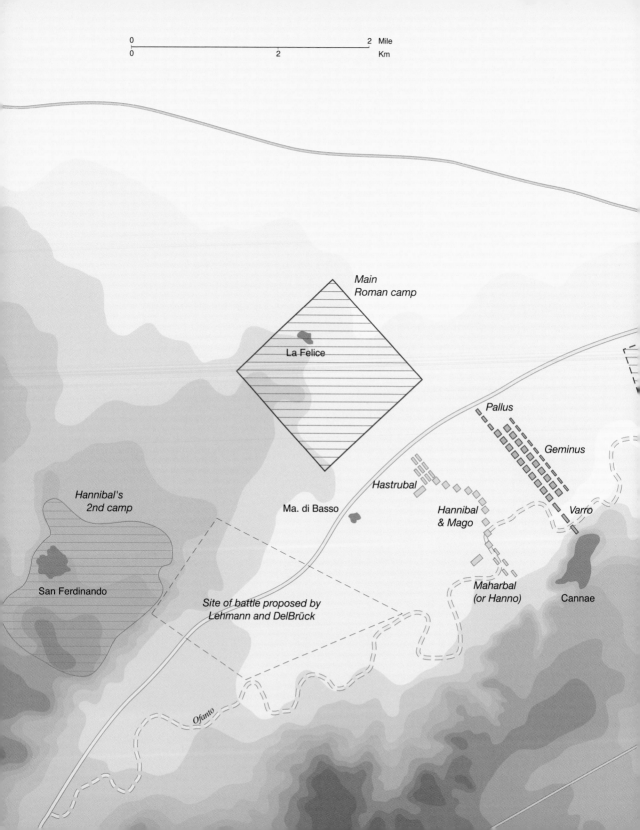

0   2   Mile
0   2   Km

*Main
Roman camp*

La Felice

Pallus

Geminus

Hastrubal

*Hannibal
& Mago*

Varro

*Hannibal's
2nd camp*

Ma. di Basso

San Ferdinando

*Maharbal
(or Hanno)*

Cannae

*Site of battle proposed by
Lehmann and DelBrück*

Ofanto

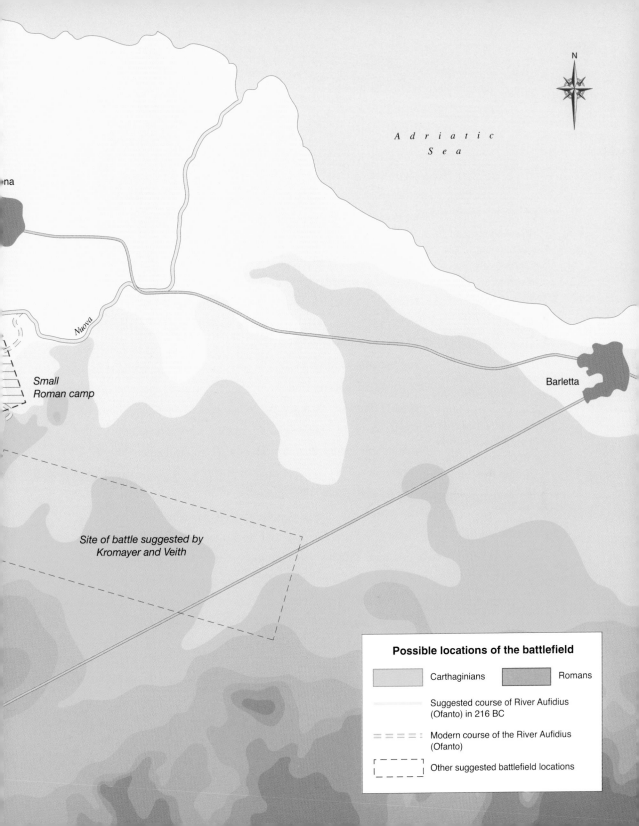

N

*A d r i a t i c
S e a*

na

Nuova

Small
Roman camp

Barletta

Site of battle suggested by
Kromayer and Veith

Possible locations of the battlefield

	Carthaginians		Romans

—— Suggested course of River Aufidius
(Ofanto) in 216 BC

= = = = Modern course of the River Aufidius
(Ofanto)

⌐ ‾ ‾ ⌐ Other suggested battlefield locations

hampered by a strong wind blowing towards them. Although doubtless exaggerated, the prevailing wind in this area is the hot Volturnus, which blows in very strong gusts from the south-west, again suggesting that the Romans faced south or south-west. The Greek historian seems to have believed that the River Aufidius flowed from south to north. In fact it runs more south-west to north-east, but meanders considerably. The general direction of the river's flow cannot have been any different in the third century BC, but its actual course is far less clear. During the last century the line of the Ofanto has changed on numerous occasions, sometimes even varying from year to year. The contours of the shallow valley through which it flows impose a northernmost and southern-most restriction, but in places this would still permit a variation of several kilometres. As a result, one of our few fixed points on the battlefield proves to be far less certain than we might like.[4]

Previous page:
The actual site of the
battlefield of Cannae
is not known with absolute certainty and must be deduced from the fragments of information provided in our sources and examination of the topography of the area. For the reasons given in the text, this assumes that the river ran further north in 216 and that the battle was fought in the position marked.

So much has been written about Cannae that it is unsurprising that the site of the battle has proved one source of major controversy. In many cases arguments have focused on minor details, but other disputes have been much deeper. The most fundamental question is on which side of the river the battle was fought, since this determines our understanding of the orientation of the battlefield. In recent years very few scholars have argued for a location on the left, or western bank, but in the past a number of eminent scholars have advocated this view, notably Hans Delbrück and Konrad Lehmann. If the battle was fought on the left bank, then the Romans – given that their right flank rested on the river – must have formed up facing towards the sea. There are several problems with this. In the first place it is very difficult to see how Polybius can have believed that the Roman line was facing south, even with his misunderstanding of the river's orientation. Secondly, for the Romans to have been camped to the west and Hannibal to the east, nearer the sea would suggest a very different build-up to the battle to the most obvious reading of our sources. It is hard to see how the armies could have ended up in this position if the Romans had followed Hannibal to Cannae from the area around Gerunium. Advocates of this view sought explanation in the problematic chronology for the campaign mentioned in the last chapter. If Hannibal left winter quarters at Gerunium when the harvest became available in early June and the battle was not fought until 2 August, then there was plenty of time – nearly two months – for more manoeuvring than is described by our sources. It was possible for Hannibal to have crossed the Aufidius and raided more widely in Apulia, before turning back north, or north-east, to seize Cannae. During this expedition he was followed by the Roman army which kept to the high ground and avoided contact. Only when the consuls had joined did the Romans choose to close the distance and a battle occur. Adherents to this cause suggest that the consuls deliberately chose a narrow battlefield west of the town of Cannae and north of the river, believing that this would protect their flanks from the superior Punic cavalry. They add that the fact that Roman fugitives from the battle gathered at Canusium would make far more sense if their army had deployed to the west of the Carthaginians.[5]

Whilst it is just possible that our sources skimmed over more than a month of operations and that the battle occurred in this way, this does seem unlikely. It is also difficult to see what useful purpose Hannibal would have served by marauding about southern Apulia. His aim in this campaign was to bring the Roman army to battle and to destroy it. The reluctance of the proconsuls throughout the winter to risk serious engagement and their care to follow him at a safe distance when he finally left Gerunium must have made it clear that there was little chance of joining battle until the new consuls arrived. With the supplies captured at Cannae, and the ease of foraging in the surrounding area, there was really no need for a mobile campaign further south. Hannibal had already demonstrated the Romans' inability to prevent his going wherever he wished. The ability of the Roman legions at Trebia to retreat to Placentia even though the enemy army lay in between suggests that we should be cautious about making too much of the routes taken by fugitives.

In addition the terrain to the north of the Aufidius fits rather better our sources' description of the Roman march towards Cannae across open country than any possible route from the south-west. On balance, it is far more likely that the battle was fought on the right, or southern, bank of the Aufidius and that the Romans had their backs to the sea and faced roughly south-east. In all of the chapters of this book I have assumed that this was the case and that therefore the larger Roman camp was on the left bank and the smaller camp on the right.

In recent years the River Ofanto has tended to run fairly close to the line of hills on which sits Cannae itself. Many scholars have assumed that there could not possibly have been sufficient space in the plain between the two to accommodate the armies, especially the huge Roman force. J. Kromayer, who assisted by G. Veith, produced in the early twentieth century what is still the classic study of the battlefields of the ancient world, therefore placed the battle to the east of Cannae itself, on the broad plain which slopes very gently down to the sea. This area is certainly wide enough to permit the deployment of nearly 140,000 men. In this interpretation the smaller Roman camp was little more than 4km from the sea and the Roman battle line a short distance in front of it. The left wing of Hannibal's army would have been fairly close to the edge of the hill of Cannae itself. His camp is unlikely to have been as far to the east as the high ground around San Ferdinando di Púglia, but would have been somewhere on the open plain north of Cannae. There could have been no intrinsic value to such a position apart from the pressure it applied on the enemy by its proximity to their camp.[6]

However, this battlefield is no less open and suitable for cavalry than the one north of the river where Paullus refused to fight on 1 August. It is difficult to understand why Varro would have made the effort of shifting the bulk of his forces across the river to the right bank to fight on virtually identical terrain. Only the Roman right flank resting on the river would have been secure, since the left had no terrain feature to anchor itself upon. In addition the slope, although gentle, would have placed the Romans at a slight, but not insignificant disadvantage. If the Roman army had decided to fight in this position on 2 August then the criticisms levelled at Varro would seem to be valid, for this area offered far more advantages to Hannibal's cavalry than it did to the Romans. Just about the only reason why the consul might have chosen to move to such a position was an urge to challenge the enemy's dominance of this bank and the area around the Roman camp which had been threatened by the Numidians the day before. The problems were not solely confined to one side, for wherever Hannibal's camp lay his columns would have had to march through an awkward little defile around the hill of Cannae in order to reach the battlefield. This would have made his deployment a more difficult and time consuming process, and a good commander tried to ensure that his troops entered battle as fresh as possible.

Both of these interpretations assumed that the Aufidius flowed on virtually the same line in 216 BC as it did in the early twentieth century. As we have seen, it is in fact perfectly possible that it followed a very different course. Assuming that the Aufidius actually lay much nearer to the northernmost limit, Peter Connolly suggested that the battle was in fact fought north of the line of hills around Cannae on a plain about 2km (*c.* 1.3 miles) in width. In order to fit such a large Roman force, whose probable frontage he calculated at around 3km (*c.* 2 miles), into this area, Connolly argued that the Romans deployed at an angle, so that in fact they were close to facing south as Polybius described. This looks a little awkward on his maps, but it should be noted that his estimate for the Roman frontage is too high as we shall see in the next section. It is much easier to fit the Roman army into this position than at first appears. The advantages of this position are obvious. The Romans were able to anchor one flank on the river and the other on the high ground near Cannae, making it impossible for the Carthaginian horse to envelop their line as they had at Ticinus and Trebia. It would make far more sense for Varro to have chosen to offer battle here, rather than simply crossing the river further east to fight in a plain very little different from the one outside the main camp.[7]

INITIAL DEPLOYMENT

Polybius tells us that the Roman army at Cannae numbered about 80,000 infantry and just over 6,000 cavalry. The figure for the infantry was clearly based on the assumption that there were eight legions of 5,000 foot supported by the same number of allied soldiers. Whether all of the legions and *alae* were in fact at this theoretical strength on 2 August is questionable, but this figure probably provides a reasonable approximation of the army's size. If all of the legions had their full complement of 300 cavalry then there should have been 2,400 Roman horse at the battle. The remaining 3,600 or so men were allied cavalry. Normally the allies provided three times as many cavalrymen as the Romans, but this did not occur in the extraordinary circumstances of 216 BC. One of Livy's sources stated that in this year the allies provided twice as many cavalry as the Romans.[8] This may simply have been a rough approximation, but it is possible that not all of the legions were able to recruit the full 300 horsemen and that as a result more of the 6,000 were allied cavalry. Despite the great effort mounted for this campaign, the overall proportion of cavalry in the army was lower than in most other Roman field armies. This may well reflect the casualties suffered in earlier engagements, notably the defeat of Centenius in 217. Another problem which doubtless restricted the number of cavalry with the army was the difficulty of finding so many mounts at such short notice.[9]

Battle scene showing Greek hoplites from the Nereid Monument in the British Museum. This relief depicting a battle between phalanxes of Greek hoplites demonstrates the problems of showing a massed battle in a two dimensional medium. The formations are shown with men standing one behind the other and there is no attempt to indicate the files of men on either side. This problem would recur in many famous works of art, for instance in the Bayeux Tapestry.

Not all of the Roman army was deployed for battle: 10,000 men were left outside the main camp. As yet the Romans did not know whether Hannibal would accept their offer of battle and transfer his army to the right bank of the Aufidius. Polybius tells us that this was Paullus' decision and that, whilst they would also guard the baggage, this force was intended to pose a threat to Hannibal's camp. This would either persuade Hannibal to weaken his army by leaving a strong garrison or, if he did not, allow the Romans to storm the Punic encampment. The loss of baggage, equipment, supplies and camp followers would have been a fatal blow, impossible for Hannibal's army to recover from if his army failed to win an outright and overwhelming victory. The attribution of this plan to Paullus once again challenges the tradition that he was less aggressive than his colleague. It is unknown who provided this force of 10,000 men, and whether it consisted of detachments from some or all of the units in the camp or of complete units. Some cavalrymen are mentioned in this camp in the aftermath of the battle which, if they were not fugitives, suggests that the covering force included both horse and foot. It has sometimes been suggested that these men were the *triarii* from the entire army, since 600 men from each of the eight legions and a similar number from the *alae* would total 9,600 men. There are a few recorded occasions when the *triarii* were given the task of protecting the army's baggage, but there is no indication that this was standard practice. Given the aggressive role planned for this force by Paullus, the *triarii* would not seem the most suitable men to carry this out, for they were not normally used as a strike force. It would also have meant sending some men from the smaller camp which seems rather unlikely. A much more plausible solution would be to see the 10,000 as one legion supported by an *ala*, but certainty is impossible. Appian, whose account of the battle is generally unreliable and confused, claims that 3,000 men were left as a covering force for the smaller camp. This may have been the case, but this position faced no immediate threat given that the main army was deployed in front of it. It may be that the semi-armed servants and camp followers there were considered sufficient protection, but once again we have no clear information.[10]

When Varro had united the two sections of the Roman army he formed them into battle formation with the Roman cavalry on the right, the Roman and allied heavy infantry in the centre and the allied horse on the left. Probably, as we have seen, his flanks rested on the river and the high ground around Cannae. There is little or no information on the formations normally employed by Roman cavalry in this period. Polybius, in a criticism of another historian's account of Alexander the Great's victory at the battle of Issus, claims that if they were to be effective then cavalry should never be deployed in more than eight ranks. He also states that wide intervals between squadrons were essential to provide them with the freedom to manoeuvre, so that when formed eight deep 800 cavalrymen occupied a frontage of 1 *stadium* (roughly a furlong), which works out at about 2m (*c.* 6–7 feet) per horseman. This is probably rather too generous for the Roman cavalry wings at Cannae. At no stage during the battle are either the Roman or allied cavalry recorded as having mounted a serious attack. They were heavily outnumbered and their role seems to have been merely to protect the flanks of the infantry and prevent them from being outflanked by the enemy horse. In such a defensive role there was no need to maintain such large intervals between squadrons or to form only eight ranks deep. In fact some of the Roman cavalry may even have dismounted and fought on foot, although the tradition is rather confused over this point. Allowing 1.5m (5 feet) per horseman and assuming that the 2,400 Roman cavalrymen on the right flank were formed ten deep, then they will have occupied a frontage of 360m and a depth of perhaps 40m. Employing the same calculation, the 3,600 allied cavalry on the left would have needed 540m by 40m.[11]

As far as we can tell, the Roman legions and allied *alae* deployed in the normal triplex *acies*. However, Polybius specifically tells us that Varro ordered two major changes from the normal drill, reducing the gaps between the maniples in each line and making each maniple very deep, so that each was 'many times deeper than it was wide'. The standard size of a maniple of *hastati* or *principes* in a normal legion was 120 men, but we do not know whether there was a standard formation for this unit. Polybius' statement here, as well as practical utility, suggests that a maniple was not normally formed with greater depth than frontage. If the Romans preferred to have equal numbers in each rank then a formation of twenty men wide by six deep or fifteen men by eight deep would be prime candidates. If each legionary was allocated a frontage of 1m (*c.* 3 feet) and a depth of 2m (6–7 feet) then the maniple would cover 20m by 12m or 15m by 16m respectively. The scant evidence for the formations of the later professional army suggest systems of drill based upon multiples of three or four, the latter being standard for Hellenistic armies. However, it is possible that the third century BC Roman army had no standard system of drill and that the depths of maniples was determined for each battle by a legion's or an army's commanders, as had been the case with most Greek hoplite armies.[12]

The legions at Cannae were unusually large with 5,000 foot apiece. Polybius tells us that when the size of a legion was increased, the number of *triarii* always remained the same at 600. The remaining 4,400 men were supposed to be divided equally between the *hastati*, *principes* and *velites*, giving each approximately 1,466 men. This would give an average strength for a maniple in the first two lines as about 146 men. If there were in fact seven legions and seven *alae* making up the line, allowing for one of each left in the larger camp, this would give 20,524 men in each of the first two lines and 8,400 in the third, a total of 49,448, supported by 20,524 *velites*. Such a strong force of light infantry ought to have given the Romans a distinct advantage in the skirmishing at the beginning of the battle, and, although there may be other reasons why this was not the case, it is possible that there were fewer *velites*. We know so little about the internal organization of the *alae* that it is impossible to say whether in fact these included roughly the same proportion of light infantry as the legions. It is also possible that, as in so many other respects in the 216 campaign, the normal procedures had been modified and the legions were themselves composed differently. In either case perhaps we should reduce the number of skirmishers by several thousand and add these to the heavy infantry. Most commentators on the battle estimate the number of close order infantrymen at around the 50,000 to 55,000 mark, but precision is impossible.[13]

We do not know precisely how deep the Roman centre was at Cannae, and various suggestions have been made, usually ranging from about fifty to seventy ranks. In some cases the lower figure has been based upon the

assumption that the *triarii* were left in the main camp. Polybius' statement that the maniples were 'many times' deeper than wide is fairly vague, but it is difficult to see it being applied to a formation much wider than five or six files across and less deep than twenty-nine or twenty-four ranks. If we assume that each maniple had a frontage of five men and a depth of twenty-nine then it would have occupied an area of 5m by 58m. The gaps between maniples in the same line were normally equivalent to the frontage of a single maniple, but at Cannae this was significantly reduced. Assuming an interval equal to half the width of a maniple, then the ten maniples of *hastati* in one legion at Cannae would have occupied about 75m by 58m, and the entire first line of the army about 1,050m by 58m. To cover the same frontage the *principes* would have been in an identical formation, but the less numerous *triarii* formed around ten to twelve deep, giving a total depth to the Roman centre of perhaps seventy-four ranks. If those scholars who suggest a somewhat shallower formation of around fifty ranks are closer to the mark, then the frontage of the infantry centre would have to be expanded to around 1.5km.

This scene from the altar of Domitius Ahenobarbus shows animals waiting to be sacrificed. In the centre are two legionary infantrymen, who could easily represent troops from any of the three lines of heavy infantry in the legions at Cannae. To the right a cavalryman stands in front of his horse.

The Roman centre at Cannae concentrated an exceptionally large number of men on a very narrow frontage and it is important to understand why such an unorthodox deployment was adopted. In any formation only the legionaries in the front rank could effectively employ their weapons. Soldiers armed with long spears might be able to reach the enemy from the second rank, but only the *triarii* at Cannae were equipped in this way. Men in the ranks behind the first could throw missiles over the men in front, although restricted visibility must have made it difficult to aim and it was a question of hoping to hit somewhere in the enemy mass. The *pilum*, the heavy throwing spear carried by legionaries and perhaps some allied soldiers, had a maximum range of just under 30m and was most effective at about half that distance. Therefore any soldiers in the ranks behind the eighth in a Roman maniple would have had difficulty in throwing their *pila* without running the risk of hitting their own front ranks. A deep formation did not offer the most effective use of a unit's weaponry which could best be served by a much shallower formation of perhaps two or three ranks, with the front rank to do the actual fighting and the others to replace casualties. Yet such shallow formations were exceedingly rare and most military theorists felt four ranks to be the minimum and recommended six or eight. Shallow formations tended inevitably to be wide and the wider a unit's frontage, the harder it was to move across the battlefield at any speed and remain in formation. A broader formation encountered more obstacles, since no battlefield was ever perfectly flat, and required a good standard of drill and the close supervision of its officers to prevent a unit from falling into disorder. As a result, over any distance, a narrower, deeper column would move more quickly whilst retaining its order than a wider, shallow line.

There were other reasons why troops tended to fight in deeper formations, which went beyond the purely practical. A column many ranks deep was an intimidating sight as it approached the enemy, even if many of the men within it would not actually be able to fight. As importantly, the close proximity of their comrades all around them encouraged the men forming the column.

There appears to be a strong herd instinct within human beings, so that even today there is a marked tendency for men under fire to bunch together for mutual comfort, despite the fact that this tends to make them more of a target. Only rigorous training has proved able to control this instinctive reaction. The physical presence of their comrades encouraged men, but also made it difficult for them to flee. The front rank could not run until all the other ranks behind them had given way. The men in the centre and rear of the formation were removed from actual physical danger in direct relation to the depth of the formation. Deeper formations did not fight any better than shallow formations, but they did possess longer endurance in combat, simply because it was that much more difficult for the actual fighting men in front to escape. Greek military theorists recommended placing the best and bravest soldiers in the front and rear ranks, the former to do the actual fighting and the latter to prevent the rest of the unit from escaping. We cannot be sure whether or not they had this function in the third century BC, but in the latter Roman army the centurions' second in command, the *optiones*, were stationed at the rear of a century to prevent the men from running away, if necessary physically forcing them back into place with their symbol of office, the *hastile* staff. An especially deep formation was one way of keeping questionable troops in the battle for a longer period, increasing the chance that the enemy's morale would crack first. Throughout the ancient world, and indeed for much later military history when troops continued to fight in close formation, there was a direct link between the quality of troops and the depth of their formation. Highly trained and well motivated soldiers were able to fight in much shallower formations than was ever possible for less experienced and poorly drilled units.[14]

The inexperience and lack of training of much of the Roman army at Cannae in part explains the decision to form them in such depth. It would have been exceptionally difficult to keep together a more conventional and shallower *triplex acies* formation, with each of the three lines stretching for several kilometres. The reduction in the frontage of each maniple and even more importantly of the intervals between them removed much of the manipular formation's flexibility, but it did make it possible to move so many men in a more co-ordinated manner. The great depth also gave the Roman infantry phenomenal staying power, making it extremely difficult, if not impossible, for an enemy to defeat them in a straightforward frontal attack. Finally we must remember that the Romans' formation may have been limited by the ground chosen for the battle. According to the above calculations, the entire Roman army occupied a frontage of about 2km or 2,100 yards (360m for the Roman cavalry, 1,050m for the infantry centre, and 540m for the allied cavalry = 1,950m). Precision cannot be claimed for a figure based upon so many conjectures and assumptions, but even if this is something of an under-estimate it would still suggest that the Roman army was more than capable of being fitted into the area between Cannae and the presumed more northern course of the Aufidius. Delbrück and Lehmann, the chief advocates of a battle-field on the left bank, similarly calculated the frontage of the Roman army as under 2km in which case it could have fitted into a plain between two phys-ical obstacles which protected its flanks.[15]

The Roman plan for the battle was simple and unsubtle, but not unreason-able or by any means inevitably doomed to failure. At Trebia a large section of the Roman legions had cut their way straight through the Punic centre, defeating not just Gallic warriors, but also the Africans, Hannibal's best infantry. At Trasimene, in spite of the massively unfavourable position and lack of organization, the Roman heavy infantry had held off the enemy attacks for hours and inflicted significant losses upon them. Throughout the same period, the Roman and allied cavalry had performed consistently badly, winning only a few minor engagements. In this battle the Romans were once again outnumbered in cavalry, but had a massive advantage in infantry. It was therefore logical to rely most upon their foot in the coming battle. The problem they faced was how to bring the weight of their infantry to bear without exposing its flanks to Hannibal's superior and mobile cavalry which had so easily swept around the Roman flanks at Trebia and robbed them of any real advantage gained by breaking the enemy centre. The answer, and it seems the reason why Varro chose to fight on the opposite bank of the River Aufidius to where Hannibal had offered battle, was to deploy not in a wide open plain, but in a narrower, more confined space. In this way the left wing was protected by the hills around Cannae and the right by the river. Although heavily outnumbered, the Roman and allied horse could not be outflanked and the enemy cavalry would be forced to attack and defeat them in a frontal charge. The Roman wings were not required to beat the enemy, but simply to stay in position for as long as possible. They were there to give sufficient time for the massed infantry in the centre to deliver an overwhelming hammer blow against Hannibal's foot. If the Punic centre could be overwhelmed, then it would matter little if the Roman wings at last gave way, for on their own the Carthaginian cavalry would not be able to do much more than harass the legions. The selection of the ground at Cannae was intended to allow the heavy infantry to smash their Punic counterparts. We do not know whether Varro alone or perhaps with the assistance of Paullus, Geminus or some of the other experienced men with the army conceived this plan. It was not complicated or especially imaginative, and in fact the very close formation of the Roman foot sacrificed the usual tactical flexibility of the legions. Elsewhere Polybius commented that the Romans as a race tended to rely instinctively on 'brute force' (*bia*) when making war and that sometimes this had led to terrible disasters. Their plan at Cannae would seem to be a prime example of this trait.[16]

The cavalry wings were the vulnerable spots, for they needed to remain in place long enough for the infantry to win. This was always going to be difficult, for infantry combats seem usually to have lasted for hours, whereas cavalry encounters were faster and more fluid. It was no coincidence that the two consuls took direct command of the wings, Varro leading the allies on the left and Paullus the Romans on the right. That Paullus was stationed with the citizen cavalry rather than the allies has been one of the chief arguments put forward for claiming that it was he who held overall command on 2 August, since it is assumed that this was a more prestigious post than controlling the non-citizen allies. This is in fact extremely tenuous, for there does not appear

A closer view of the soldiers on the altar of Domitius Ahenobarbus. All three wear mail shirts like that depicted on the Gallic warrior from Vachères. Those of the two infantrymen have clearly depicted doubling on their shoulders. Both men carry heavy semi-cylindrical shields with barleycorn shaped bosses either of wood or bronze. Their helmets are probably of Attic or Etrusco-Corinthian pattern.

to have been any set place from which a Roman consul was supposed to lead the army. Most certainly there was no convention for where each consul should be when both were present with the army, for this was such a rare event. Roman generals tended to station themselves wherever they felt that they could do most to influence the battle and thus usually where they anticipated its crisis to occur, hence the consuls' presence with the cavalry at

Cannae. The centre was placed under the command of Servilius Geminus. There were also many tribunes and prefects, so that the Roman and allied foot were led by a very large number of senior officers concentrated along a small frontage. We do not know how the legions and *alae* were arranged. Livy says that the Roman legions were on the right and the allied foot on the left, but it is hard to know what to make of this. Conventionally the legions held the centre and the *alae* were split on either side,

A relief depicting an Iberian cavalryman from Osuna in Spain. Much detail has been lost but he clearly carries a short sword. A good number of Hasdrubal's heavy cavalry on the left wing were Spanish.

but there was no precedent for an eight legion army to know whether this would be followed in these circumstances. One possibility is that the different armies formed up side by side, so that the legions and *alae* used to working with each other remained together. One attractive idea is that the centre of the line was formed by the proconsuls' forces, so that the best and most experienced troops formed the heart of the Roman attack, but once again this is purely conjectural. Whatever the precise details, the unprecedentedly large Roman host can only have presented an intimidating sight to the watching Carthaginians.[17]

The Romans could not be sure that Hannibal would accept their offer of battle in this confined position, hence the strong force left outside the larger camp. It is even possible that Varro did not expect the Carthaginian to fight and saw this largely as a morale boosting operation for his own soldiers, rebuilding their confidence after the humiliation of the day before. This is certainly possible for such gestures were common before the battles of this period, but it is far more probable that the Romans did want to fight the battle on this ground of their own choosing. Whatever their intentions, the sources

imply that Hannibal ordered his army to move out almost as soon as he saw Varro's columns leaving the main camp. The Carthaginian sent out his light troops to form a protective screen for the main body. This was standard practice for most armies and it is more than probable that the complicated process of forming up the Roman army was carried out behind a line of *velites* and perhaps some of the cavalry. Polybius noted that Hannibal's army crossed the Aufidius at two points, which makes it very likely that it was divided into two columns for deployment. The Carthaginians then formed into battle order, probably within a kilometre of the Roman line.[18]

The initial deployment of the two armies at Cannae, shown to scale under the assumption that the River Aufidius ran further north in 216. Each army occupied a frontage of some two kilometres, cramming some 130,000 men into a narrow valley, but giving the Romans secure flanks. Hannibal's formation made best use of the differing qualities of his soldiers.

Hannibal is said to have had 10,000 cavalry and 40,000 infantry at Cannae, but we have no precise figures for the various contingents making up this total. The cavalry were a mixture of Spanish and Gallic horse, both of whom fought in close order, and the Numidian light cavalry. The Gauls had all been recruited from the Cisalpine tribes after Hannibal arrived in Italy and he is said to have had 6,000 Spanish and Numidian horse after crossing the Alps. At most the Numidians may have accounted for two thirds of this total, but they must have suffered some casualties in the 218 and 217 campaigns and their strength was probably somewhere between 3,000 and 4,000. At Cannae the Numidians were placed on the Punic right flank opposite Varro and the Allied cavalry and it seems probable that they roughly equalled these in numbers. All of the Gallic and Spanish cavalry, some 6,000–7,000 men, were massed on the left flank, giving them a numerical superiority of two or three to one over their Roman counterparts. Probably the Punic horse occupied roughly the same frontage as the Roman and allied cavalry, but it is unlikely that they were quite so densely packed. The Numidians normally fought in small, widely spread bodies which advanced and retreated in each other's support, always avoiding close contact but harassing the enemy with missiles. The Gauls and Spaniards were almost certainly divided into several lines of squadrons, for if

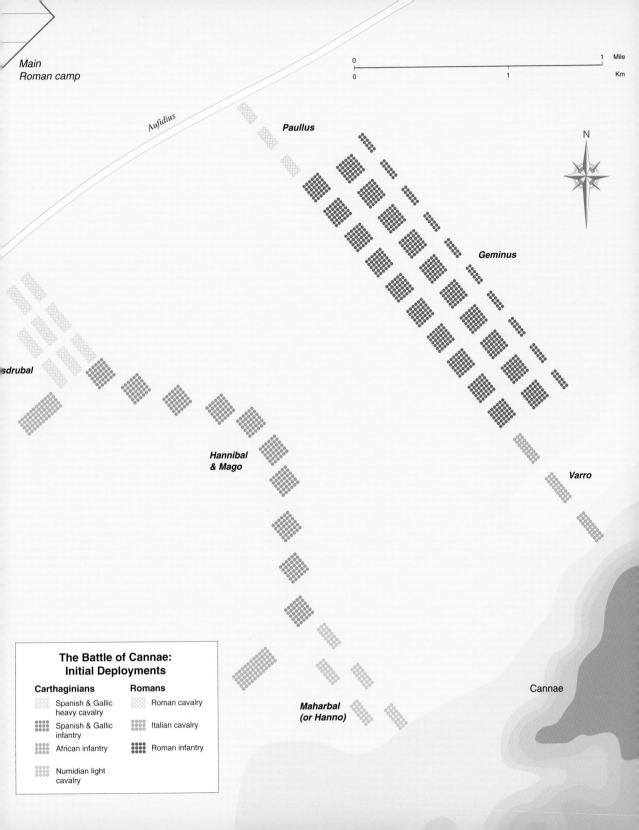

Main
Roman camp

Aufidius

Paullus

Geminus

Hasdrubal

Hannibal
& Mago

Varro

Maharbal
(or Hanno)

Cannae

0   1   Mile

0   1   Km

N

The Battle of Cannae:
Initial Deployments

Carthaginians   **Romans**

Spanish & Gallic   Roman cavalry
heavy cavalry

Spanish & Gallic   Italian cavalry
infantry

African infantry   Roman infantry

Numidian light
cavalry

cavalry became too crowded then they tended to merge into one mass which was difficult for its leaders to control and inclined to panic and stampede. The behaviour of these horsemen during the battle makes it clear that they were kept closely in hand by their officers.

Hannibal's infantry were formed with the African foot on the flanks and the Gauls and Spanish in the centre. It is difficult to know how many men should be deducted from the total of 40,000 to account for the infantry skirmishers. He had had 8,000 of these men at Trebia and although his army had been significantly augmented by Gallic tribesmen since then it is questionable how many skirmishers these provided. The warrior culture of the Gallic tribes placed most emphasis on close fighting and light infantry seem to have played little part in inter-tribal warfare. If there were still only 8,000 light troops at Cannae, then the close order foot mustered something like 32,000 men, once again divided into Gauls, Africans and Spanish. Hannibal had 20,000 foot when he arrived in Italy, consisting of the Libyans, Spanish and light infantry, and none of these contingents had as yet received any reinforcements. Perhaps there were around 6,000 light infantry, some of them Spanish, 4,000 Spanish close order troops and 10,000 Libyans. All of these had suffered some casualties by August 216. If there were 8,000–9,000 Libyans and around 3,000–4,000 Spanish at Cannae, then that would suggest something like 19,000–21,000 Gallic warriors in the main line.

The Carthaginian centre consisted of the Gallic and Spanish foot, perhaps 24,000 men in all. These were intermingled, companies or units of each being deployed alternately. Polybius uses the Greek word *speirai* (spe…rai) for these units, a term which he also sometimes employs for the Roman maniple and which would later become the term used for the 480 man cohort adopted by the professional Roman army. It is doubtful that these bands were of uniform size, and anyway either there must have been more Gallic than Spanish units or each unit was significantly larger, but it is most likely that this refers to a group of a few hundred men and probably less than a thousand. The African foot were divided into two roughly equal bodies and stationed on the flanks near the cavalry. They were formed either in one deep column or in several lines one behind the other. Although this is not explicitly stated by any of our sources, it is highly probable that the Libyans were in fact behind the main line of Gauls and Spanish and concealed from the Romans' view. The likelihood is that they formed one of the two columns used by the Punic army in its deployment. The Africans, issued by Hannibal with captured Roman equipment, were approximately equivalent in size to two legions, one behind each of the Carthaginian army's flanks.[19]

Once all the units of the army were in place, Hannibal made one major alteration to its formation, advancing the units in the centre of the main line so that this bulged towards the enemy. The most probable interpretation of the descriptions in our sources is that the companies in the very centre of the line advanced to form a line further forward and that the companies on either side were echeloned back. It must have been obvious that the Romans were relying on the densely packed mass of infantry in their centre to win the battle. Hannibal's foot were greatly outnumbered and in the past had had difficulty standing up to the legions even on equal terms. At Trebia Hannibal's foot had formed a single line so that there were no reserves to plug the gap when the Romans broke through his centre. At Cannae he could have chosen to make his centre as strong as possible by concentrating all the foot into one line. Yet he could not rival the depth and therefore the endurance of the Roman infantry and in the end such a line was likely to give way. Another option would have been to copy Roman practice and divide the foot into two or more lines stationed one behind the other, so that as the troops in the fighting line became weary they could be reinforced by fresh reserves, something Hannibal would choose to do at Zama in 202 BC. However, once again, this could at best delay the inevitable Roman breakthrough. Instead of delaying the clash with this overwhelming force, Hannibal kept his centre relatively shallow and then moved it forward so that the Roman charge would reach it more quickly. His objective was to concentrate the Roman effort at the very centre of his line, knowing that it must inevitably break and that the Romans would pour through the gap they had created. Then, it was hoped, they might make themselves vulnerable to flank attacks from the Libyan foot, his best, most disciplined men. Whilst this was going on the Numidians on the left were supposed to keep the Latin cavalry busy, and at the same time the concentrated force of the Gallic and Spanish horse mounted a huge, direct attack at the Roman right. These were to smash the Roman cavalry and then, remaining in good order, threaten the rear of the Roman army.[20]

In essence Hannibal hoped to use the Romans' own strength against them, drawing them in to be surrounded and destroyed. It was a complex plan, contrasting sharply with the brutally simple tactics of the enemy. It also made very heavy demands on both his soldiers and their officers. Hannibal himself, supported by his youngest brother Mago, took up position in the centre with the Spaniards and Gauls for it was vital that these warriors held out as long as possible. The Numidians were led by Hanno according to Polybius and Maharbal in Livy's account, whilst the vital task of leading the squadrons on the left was entrusted to Hasdrubal. The events of the battle were to demonstrate the great superiority which the Carthaginian army derived from the command structure and mutual trust between leaders and forged by years of campaigning together. In spite of this, the plan was fraught with risks and by no means as certain of success as is sometimes implied in modern accounts.

Hannibal's tactics were tailored to the specific conditions of the battle, with the Romans, and especially their infantry, deployed in great depth on an exceptionally narrow front. Over the years some highly fanciful attempts have been made to see this as the fruition of long held plans, perhaps even based on the naval battle of Ecnomus or first conceived by Hamilcar Barca, passed on to his sons and experimented with at Trebia and Ibera in 215. There is no reason to believe that either Hamilcar or his capable sons attempted to conform rigidly to previously conceived plans. It is worth considering when Hannibal decided to form his army in this way. The decision to advance the centre of the Spanish and Celts may have been made on the spot, late in the stage of the army's deployment, but the concentration of all of his heavy cavalry on the left and the positioning of the Libyan foot on the flanks must already have been decided upon before the army marched in its deployment columns out of camp. Organizing the army and issuing orders so that each contingent knew where it was supposed to be took time. It seems unlikely that Hannibal could have devised these complex tactics and the means of implementing them after he had seen the Romans begin to march out of camp and cross the river on the morning of 2 August. There was no reason for him to have formed his army in this way and on such a narrow frontage when he offered battle in the plain north of the river. Had he known that the Romans were planning to form on the narrow plain between Cannae and the river then the lack of space would have given a fairly clear idea of their likely deployment. This raises the intriguing possibility that the Carthaginians had seen Roman officers looking at the ground on the previous day – a highly likely activity if they were considering fighting on it. If this is right then it would further support the idea that Paullus, who was in command on 1 August, was far less reluctant to fight a battle than our sources suggest. In some way Hannibal does seem to have known or guessed how and where the Romans would fight and devised his plan accordingly, or perhaps his soldiers and officers were so superior to the enemy that he was able to react to the Roman plan and still form up within the time taken for the great enemy host to deploy.[21]

THE BATTLE

Opening Moves

We do not know how long it took for the two armies to march from their camps and deploy for battle, but at the very least it must have taken several hours. Throughout this process, each army's officers, especially the Roman tribunes who seem to have had a particular responsibility for overseeing the army's deployment, needed to be very active, closely regulating the columns and then ensuring that each unit ended up in the right place and correct formation. At the end of this process, something like 126,000 men and at least 16,000 horses were packed into a few square kilometres of the narrow plain between the Aufidius and the high ground near Cannae. In summer the Apulian soil is dry and the tread of so many feet and hoofs must have thrown up great clouds of fine, sandy-coloured dust to be whipped around by the sudden gusts of the Volturnus wind. A fragment of the Roman poet Ennius, who composed his epic verse history of Rome not long after the Second Punic War, appears to refer to the dust of Cannae.[22]

Each army marshalled its line behind a screen of light infantrymen and it was these troops who opened the fighting, closing to skirmish with each other. Javelins could be thrown perhaps as far as 30–40m, although their effective range is likely to have been less. Slings and bows – and there may have been a few archers at Cannae though none are specifically attested – had a range of nearer 200m, but it is much more difficult to estimate their effective range. The distance and accuracy of fire was determined far more by the skill of the individual slinger or archer than by the technological limitations of his weapon. Unlike firearms, where the missile is projected by chemical energy, a sling or bow transfers the physical strength of the operator to its projectile. Skirmish combats in this period were conducted at ranges of less than a few hundred metres and usually considerably closer. Most battles in the classical world began with such encounters, but these were very rarely described in any detail in our sources. Cannae is no exception, and we are simply told that the light infantry screens met without either side winning a significant advantage. In ideal circumstances skirmishers were supposed to drive back their opposite numbers and then begin to weaken the enemy's main line, but such successes were exceptionally rare. Even those close order troops who lacked body armour or helmets usually carried large shields which gave very good protection against thrown javelins, arrows or sling stones. It was also extremely dangerous for the light troops to get too close to a formed line for they were highly vulnerable to a sudden charge, especially if unsupported by close order infantry or cavalry of their own.[23]

It is improbable that many casualties were inflicted on either side during combats between skirmishers. Thrown and shot missiles could be delivered with accuracy and some force, but were also highly visible in flight – this was also true, though to a lesser extent, of sling bullets – and therefore comparatively easy for the target to dodge or catch on a shield. Skirmishers operated in a very loose order, with wide gaps between men to ensure that they could easily move to avoid an incoming missile. Even if a man was wounded, and the vast majority of injuries caused by such missiles would not have been fatal, then the distances involved usually ensured that he could be carried away to the rear by his comrades. Skirmish fights seem to have been able to go on for several hours, or even all day, with very few men on either side being killed and no clear result. This is a little difficult for us to imagine, although very similar to some of the long range musketry duels of the eighteenth and nineteenth centuries AD. Modern studies suggest that relatively few soldiers, even in the best trained units, actively aim at and seek to kill the enemy in combat, most firing their weapons wildly and some not even firing at all. Certainly the ratio between the number of rounds fired and the number of casualties inflicted on the enemy in the well documented combats of the last few centuries has been staggeringly low, usually at least several hundred to one. It is unlikely that, in the pressure of combat when the target was firing back, the archers, slingers and javelinmen of the ancient world did much better. The loose and fluid formation employed by skirmishers, where there were no set places in rank or file and each man was allowed great freedom to advance and retire at will, made it difficult to force men to fight properly, for it prevented an officer and his comrades from knowing precisely what a man was doing. A minority of soldiers went close to the enemy and sought to make use of their weapons as effectively as possible, inflicting most, if not all, of the casualties. The majority did enough to appear eager, periodically going forward to perhaps within extreme range of the enemy and throwing or shooting a missile, but being more concerned to avoid being hit themselves than to harm the enemy. A minority probably stayed as far in the rear as possible, rarely if ever coming within range. The tentative nature of the fighting between the scattered skirmishers and the ease of avoiding missiles whose flight was readily visible help to explain the indecisiveness and low number of casualties in such encounters.[24]

According to our estimates for the size of the armies at Cannae, Hannibal had at least 8,000 light infantryman and the Romans perhaps as many as 20,000. It is distinctly possible that the first figure is too low and the second too high, but even so the Romans ought to have had a significant numerical advantage and we need to ask why this does not seem to have brought them more success. One reason might be that when, as discussed above, only a minority of soldiers fought effectively sheer numbers were not of decisive importance. Another possibility is that the battlefield was too small for so many loose order troops to deploy and made it impossible for the numerically superior Romans to outflank their opponents. Probably the most important reason was the greatly superior quality of Hannibal's light infantry. These included the renowned Balearic slingers, Spanish *caetrati* (warriors with light equipment and the small round shields from which they derived their name), and probably, Libyans and Numidians. The combination of slings and javelins made the Punic skirmishers effective at both long and short range and they seem to have been well trained, specialist troops. In contrast the Roman *velites* consisted of those too young to fight with the heavy infantry or too poor to afford the necessary equipment. Nearly all were armed with javelins, although it is just possible that there was also a small contingent of archers, but they do not appear to have received much training for their role. At Telamon in 225 BC the *velites* had performed very well, although significantly they were not opposed by many enemy light troops on this occasion. In the early second century BC Roman *velites* proved themselves markedly superior to the skirmishers in eastern armies, displaying a notable willingness to close and fight hand to hand. There was no trace of similar aggression in the early years of the Second Punic War. Some have suggested that it was only after the legions

The first phase of the battle. Skirmishers ran forward from the main lines to fight a desultory skirmish in the centre. In spite of a significant numerical superiority, the Romans failed to gain any advantage. On the Punic left, nearest the river, Hasdrubal led his massed squadrons of Gallic and Spanish cavalry in a ferocious charge against the Roman cavalry.

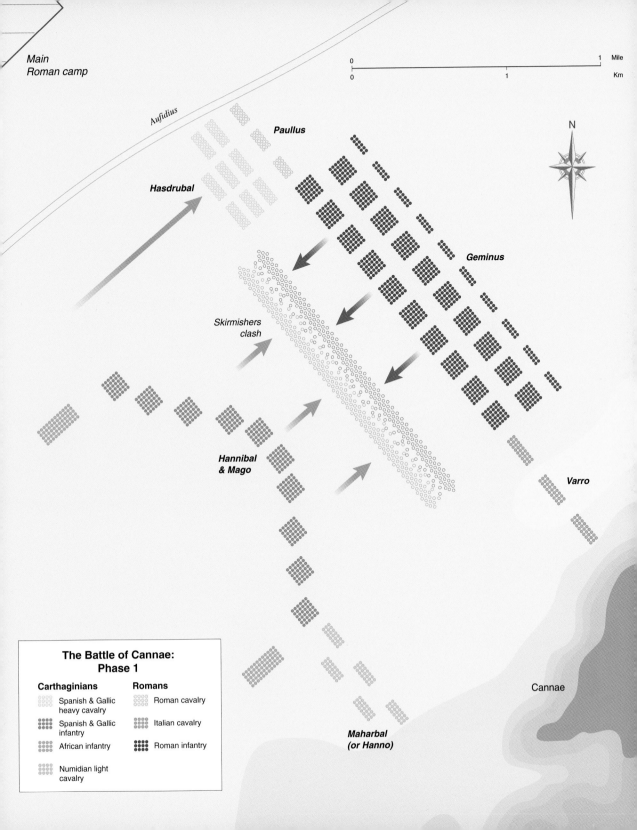

Main
Roman camp

Aufidius

0   1   Mile

0   1   Km

N

Paullus

Hasdrubal

Geminus

*Skirmishers
clash*

**Hannibal
& Mago**

Varro

Cannae

The Battle of Cannae:
Phase 1

Carthaginians   **Romans**

Spanish & Gallic   Roman cavalry
heavy cavalry

Spanish & Gallic   Italian cavalry
infantry

African infantry   Roman infantry

Numidian light
cavalry

**Maharbal
(or Hanno)**

changed the equipment and training of their light infantry in a major reform in 211 that these began to become effective troops, but there is no good evidence for this. Far more probably it was a case of the greater experience derived from service in the war with Carthage which produced the high quality *velites* of the early second century, and we should note that in every respect the legions fielded in these years were far better than their predecessors. In 216 the Roman light infantry were mostly inexperienced and had received little or no training.[25]

The Cavalry Clash on the Wings

At Trebia Hannibal had withdrawn his light infantry once they had driven in their Roman counterparts, and sent them to support his cavalry, adding to the discomfiture of the already tired and outnumbered Roman horse. It is possible that he did the same at Cannae, for later in his narrative, Livy tells us that

These heavily decorated boxes from Florence show scenes from Roman legends. On the left can be seen the figure of Marcus Curtius riding a horse and fully equipped as a cavalryman. His equipment would not have been out of place amongst the Roman and Allied cavalry at Cannae.

'at the beginning of the battle he [Paullus] had been seriously wounded by a slingstone', although this was not to stop him from continuing to lead his men. Polybius does not mention this and in fact says that, when Paullus left the defeated right wing and went to join the struggle in the centre, he was unwounded. Perhaps he meant that the consul had not suffered an incapacitating wound, which might reconcile the account with Livy's, or he had simply not heard this tradition, but it is also possible that the story was a later invention intended to add to the already heroic character of Paullus. Ultimately we cannot say precisely what happened to the Punic light infantry, or indeed the Roman *velites*, after each screen had withdrawn behind their main lines, but it seems probable that they continued to act in support of the formed troops.[26]

What is clear is that very early in the battle, and certainly before the main lines of infantry had clashed, Hasdrubal led his Spanish and Gallic horsemen in a direct charge against the Roman cavalry on the right. Normally cavalry combats were fast moving and fluid affairs. In a charge, the faster a squadron went the more its formation dissolved as faster horses with better riders outstripped the lesser mounts and less skilled horsemen and, even more importantly, the minority of bolder soldiers naturally pushed ahead of the majority of more timid men. Deep formations, with cavalry as with infantry, made it harder for men to run away, but it was very difficult to keep in close formation as the speed increased. A successful charge, especially when the victors gave in to their natural exhilaration and pursued the fleeing enemy, resulted in scattered men and tired horses. If the victors were then themselves charged by a fresh and well formed enemy squadron then it was very likely that they in turn would flee. In most cases, as with cavalry encounters in the eighteenth and nineteenth century AD, it was comparatively rare for the two sides to cross swords in a prolonged mêlée, since usually one or the other wheeled and fled before contact. Charge and pursuit was frequently followed by flight until the enemy were in turn driven back by fresh reserves and the squadron could reform. Victory normally went to the side which kept in hand a formed reserve on fresh horses after all the opposing cavalry had been committed.

The fighting at Cannae did not conform to this pattern and Polybius tells us that there was none of the normal 'wheeling about and reforming facing the original direction'. According to Livy this was because the fighting occurred in such a confined space, between the river and the flank of the Roman infantry, making it impossible for either side to outflank the other. Instead the Carthaginians attacked head on into the Roman cavalry, and the ensuing combat was described by Polybius as 'barbaric', clearly in the more general sense of the word as particularly brutal and unsophisticated rather than implying tactics peculiar to the tribal peoples. He says that many men dismounted and fought on foot as infantry. Livy's account is similar and he claims that, once the two sides had met, horsemen began to drag their opponents bodily from their seats. This was not the first occasion in the Second Punic War where our sources claim that cavalrymen dismounted to fight on foot, as Polybius and Livy both state that many riders had done this at Ticinus. It used to be thought that the ancient cavalryman's lack of stirrups gave him the most precarious of seats and as a result made him likely to fall off if he engaged actively in hand-to-hand combat. Recent trials with reconstructions of the four-horned saddle, probably already in use with all the horsemen at Cannae apart from the Numidians, have shown that in fact this provided a very secure seat and allowed a rider to deliver a range of blows, leaning to either side without losing his balance. The horsemen of this period were probably no more likely to fall off during a combat than cavalrymen equipped with stirrups. It was therefore not necessity that persuaded cavalrymen to fight on foot.[27]

Plutarch tells the story that Paullus' horse was wounded and the consul forced to dismount. His staff quickly followed suit and then all the rest of the Roman cavalry, assuming that this was a general order, also got off their horses. Seeing this, Hannibal is supposed to have said that the Romans might just as well have handed themselves over to him in chains like captives. It is not altogether clear to which phase of the battle this anecdote refers, although most probably it concerns the initial fighting on the Roman right wing. Livy tells much the same anecdote, but in this version it was weakness due to his own wounds which prevented the consul from staying on his horse and made both him and his cavalry bodyguard dismount. This occurs much later in the battle and assumes that some at least of the Roman cavalry were not swept away in the rout of the right wing and continued to follow the consul. Appian mentions another tradition which had Paullus dismounting near the end of the battle to fight to the death on foot with a group of survivors. The reliability of any of these stories is very difficult to judge and the tale of the Roman cavalry accidentally putting themselves at a disadvantage by dismounting may simply have been a Roman invention to excuse their defeat.[28]

These stories imply that the decision of some Roman cavalry to fight dismounted was either a mistake or a sign of desperation. As Hannibal's supposed comments make clear, it made little sense for cavalry to give up the mobility which was their chief advantage. What is clear from our sources is that the fighting between the Roman and Carthaginian cavalry was especially fierce and far less fluid than most cavalry combats. The Greeks and Romans associated determined, static fighting with foot rather than horse, and it is just possible that an account stating that the combat was more like an infantry than a cavalry mêlée is the source of these passages. Yet all our sources imply that the Roman cavalry did not advance any significant distance to meet the oncoming Gallic and Spanish horse and that their posture was essentially defensive. Cavalry have never been well suited to holding ground, for their advantages lie in speed and mobility. Unless very densely packed indeed and especially determined, a stationary mass of cavalry was always inclined to stampede to the rear when charged by enemy horse. There were many occasions in the ancient world when blocks of infantry were interspersed with cavalry squadrons. The foot provided firepower and, even more importantly, solid shelter for retreating squadrons to rally behind. It may be that at Cannae, some or all of the Roman horsemen were dismounted to act in this way or

The reliefs on the Arch of Orange in southern France depict a fierce battle between Romans and Gallic tribesmen. Although dating to more than 200 years after Cannae, and showing the Roman army equipment of the later period, the Gauls shown here would not have been out of place in the Second Punic War. This whirling combat may give some idea of the fighting at Cannae, where Gauls formed the majority of Hannibal's heavy cavalry and a considerable proportion of his infantry.

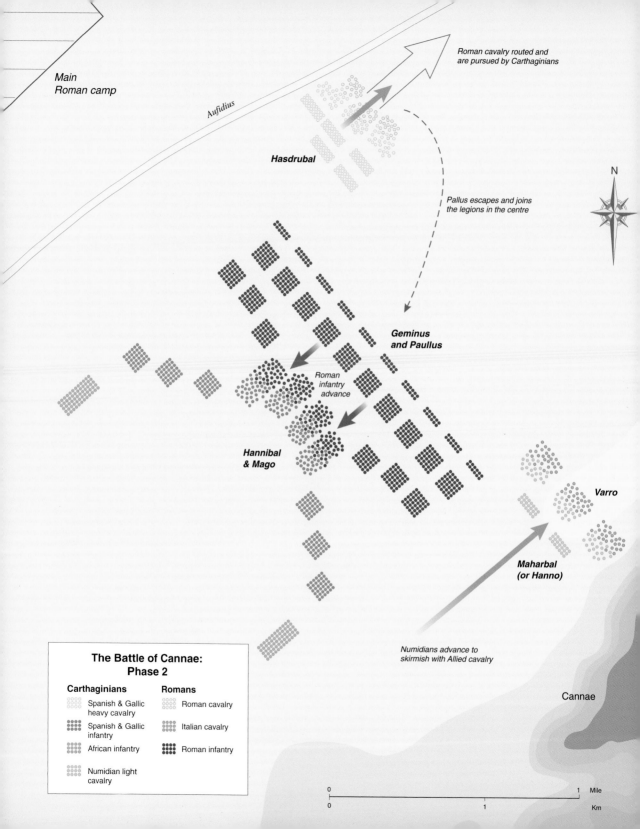

Main
Roman camp

Aufidius

Roman cavalry routed and
are pursued by Carthaginians

Hasdrubal

*Pallus escapes and joins
the legions in the centre*

N

**Geminus
and Paullus**

*Roman
infantry
advance*

**Hannibal
& Mago**

Varro

**Maharbal
(or Hanno)**

*Numidians advance to
skirmish with Allied cavalry*

Cannae

**The Battle of Cannae:
Phase 2**

Carthaginians	Romans
Spanish & Gallic heavy cavalry	Roman cavalry
Spanish & Gallic infantry	Italian cavalry
African infantry	Roman infantry
Numidian light cavalry	

0   1   Mile

0   1   Km

perhaps some detachments of ordinary infantry were interspersed with the cavalry squadrons, giving a stability to the wing which cavalry on their own would have lacked.[29] The Romans needed their cavalry wings to stay in place for long enough to prevent the Punic cavalry from threatening the main assault by the legions in the centre. The Carthaginian cavalry was known to be better than their own horse and, as the enemy deployed, it must have been clear that the Romans were heavily outnumbered on this wing. Mixing mounted with dismounted men offered the prospect of delaying a defeat which probably seemed inevitable, so that it could not affect the eventual outcome of the battle. If this was the consuls' plan, then it failed.

Livy says of the combat on the wing that 'the fight was more fierce than of long duration, and the battered Roman cavalrymen turned their backs and fled'. It is always difficult to know what to make of such vague and relative statements of time, but the Romans appear to have broken not long after the infantry centres clashed. The Roman plan required their cavalry to hold out for as long as possible so that their overwhelming assault would have time to smash through the Punic centre. Conversely Hannibal needed his left wing, where he had stationed at least two thirds of his mounted men, to rout their opponents as swiftly as possible and then return to the attack. It was Hasdrubal rather than Paullus who was best able to achieve his objective and considerable credit must go to this officer for leading his men in such a furious charge. The Carthaginians had a great numerical superiority, somewhere between two and three to one, but were probably prevented from gaining much advantage from this due to the confined space. More importantly they were better motivated and more confident than their opponents, for throughout the early years of the Second Punic War Roman cavalry had lost virtually all the engagements which they had fought. Included in the cavalry at Cannae were almost certainly some of the survivors

The second phase of the battle. After a stiff fight, Hasdrubal routed the Roman cavalry and pursued them for a short distance along the river. The consul Paullus escaped and rode to join the heavy infantry in the centre. These had moved forward and come into contact with the advanced enemy centre. There the Gauls and Spanish were fighting hard to hold back the great columns of Roman infantry, both sides being urged on by their commanders.

of the routs at Ticinus and Trebia and it is more than likely that the Roman horse had simply accustomed themselves to the idea of losing to their Carthaginian opponents. Roman horsemen were recruited from the wealthiest classes and it may be that the accounts of their determined resistance were exaggerated to please these influential citizens, something taken to an extreme by Appian who tells of them hurling back several assaults.[30]

For whatever reasons, the Roman right wing gave way and dissolved into rout. Hasdrubal's men pursued them, cutting down many of the fugitives, their flight made difficult by the shape of the river. Paullus, his staff, and perhaps some others went to join the infantry, but the majority of the Roman cavalrymen were killed or dispersed and would take no further part in the fighting. Hasdrubal exercised very tight control of his men. If, as suggested earlier, his troops had begun the battle in several lines, then only the first line may have actually been committed to the fighting and subsequent pursuit. The narrowness of the plain edged by the meandering river and the proximity of the smaller Roman camp may have helped to keep the pursuers together as well as hindering the Romans' escape. It was not long before the bulk of the Carthaginian left wing cavalry was re-formed and rested, ready to re-enter the battle.

On the opposite flank, where the Numidians faced Varro and the allied horse, the fighting had been far more tentative. These light horsemen fought in their traditional way, small groups closing to throw javelins, but rapidly retreating before the enemy could reach them with a charge. It is highly unlikely that these missiles caused significant casualties. Varro's men seem to have made little effort to drive the enemy back. Their role was simply to protect the infantry's flank and merely staying where they were achieved this satisfactorily. Livy claims that some disorder was occasioned at the very beginning of the battle when a group of 500 Numidians pretended to desert to the Romans. These men are supposed to have carried swords concealed under their body armour (which in fact the Numidians rarely, if ever, wore) and, once they were behind the Roman lines, had suddenly attacked them from the rear.

In Appian it is a group of 500 Celtiberians who employ the same ruse. It is unlikely that either story is true, but such tales of Punic treachery may have been current even in the immediate aftermath of the battle as attempts to explain the Romans' overwhelming defeat as anything other than their simply having been outfought.[31]

The Roman Centre Advances

Although Hannibal had advanced the centre of his main line to form the crescent-shaped formation before the battle, these troops do not subsequently seem to have moved any further forward. Instead, once the skirmishers had fought their indecisive combat and withdrawn through the narrow gaps in the main lines, it was the Roman infantry who attacked. Elsewhere Polybius twice tells us that it was the Roman custom at this time to advance noisily, the men cheering and clashing their weapons against their wooden shields, whilst the trumpeters carrying the curved military horn, the *cornu*, added their blare to the cacophony of noise. Visually the massed ranks of Roman infantry can only have been an intimidating sight. At a distance, and the armies may have begun up to about a kilometre apart, the small intervals between maniples were probably scarcely visible and the Roman centre must have appeared an almost solid mass of rank upon rank of armoured men behind oval shields. The legionaries and allied troops were probably not uniformed in the modern sense, since each man supplied his own equipment and we do not know for instance whether legions painted their shields in a certain colour or with a specific device, but the minor differences in appearance would only have been apparent at close range. It is probable that, like soldiers in later Roman armies, the men in 216 had taken care to dress well for a battle, polishing armour and helmets, and donning the tall crests which added to each man's apparent height. By the time that the Roman centre began to lumber forward, the men were undoubtedly covered in a thin layer of the dust, clouds of which continued to be thrown up by their marching feet and whipped around in the gusting wind.[32]

The greatly outnumbered Gauls and Spaniards watched as the grand Roman attack came straight towards them. They too raised their battle cries, clashed weapons together and blew their trumpets, including no doubt the tall *carnyx* which was said to produce an especially harsh note. Perhaps individual warriors ran a little way forward to show off their prowess and display their contempt for the enemy, for such acts of bravado were common in tribal warfare. Our sources emphasize the wild and frightening appearance of these tribesmen, the Spanish supposedly in their usual white tunics with red or purple borders, the Gauls clad in trousers but with bare torsos. The noise and displays served the same purpose for both sides. It was hard for troops to advance or wait in silence to fight a visible enemy, and shouting relieved the tension and helped the men to cope with their growing fear.

The idealized barbarian: a Gaul who has already killed his wife stabs himself. At Cannae this Roman stereotype, noble but defeated, was far from reality.

They shouted louder to show themselves that they were not truly afraid, and the more their comrades joined in the more they encouraged each other. Thus soldiers urged themselves on, whilst the noise they made and the appearance of confidence they presented would hopefully intimidate the enemy. The early phases of a battle were fought as much in the mind as with physical weapons, for if one side shouted louder and appeared more formidable then the other side's spirit declined and might even collapse. In extreme cases appearance alone was enough to convince troops that they could not win and put them to flight before a blow was struck. It was said that the German tribes could tell which way a battle would go simply by listening to the shouts raised by the rival armies.[33]

In this case both sides were highly confident and do not seem to have been unduly intimidated by the opposition. The Gauls and Spaniards had the confidence of past victories over similar Roman armies, and perhaps there was pride too, for they had been chosen from all the Punic army to be the first to meet the enemy's main attack. This was an opportunity to prove their courage in plain view and may have exploited a similar urge to the one which had led the naked Gaesatae to run out ahead of the main line and challenge the enemy at Telamon in 225 BC. The advancing Romans trusted to the superiority of their numbers, but some may have remembered that even in their recent defeats legionaries had often prevailed over such unarmoured warriors. Both sides were encouraged by the many officers in or near the front of the formation, moving around and urging on the soldiers.[34]

Eventually the Romans came within range of missiles. Tests with reconstructed *pila* suggest that this heavy throwing spear had a maximum range of between 25 and 30m, and effective range of about half that distance. Other javelins, including those probably used by the Gauls and some of the Spaniards, may have had a slightly, but not substantially longer range. Whether all soldiers waited until they were within the most effective range before throwing their *pilum* or javelin is highly questionable. Modern studies of combat suggest that only a minority of soldiers actually fired their personal weapon during a firefight and that even fewer did so with care and took trouble to aim. Both sides had been yelling for some time, nervously watching as the gap separating their own and the enemy's line grew narrower. Shouting helped them to fight against their fear, but the urge to do something to strike at and frighten off the approaching enemy must have been overwhelming. Throwing a missile at that enemy was the best way of striking at and perhaps driving off the foe.

In the later, professional Roman army, the tactical doctrine was to advance slowly, in good order, and complete silence towards the enemy. Then, probably within 15m – the *pilum*'s effective range – they delivered a devastating volley of *pila* and immediately charged, at last breaking their silence to yell out a war cry and letting the trumpets blare. The first century AD Jewish historian Josephus, who gives us our only account from a non-Roman of what it was like to face such an attack, spoke of the terrifying moment when legionaries finally broke their silence and charged. This method of fighting required an immensely high level of discipline which was only the product of good training. Even so, there appear to have been cases when this discipline was not enough and the attack was not pressed, degenerating instead to a more sporadic exchange of missiles. Most armies in the third century BC, and especially the legions at Cannae, simply did not have this level of training. Polybius tells us that each legionary carried two *pila*, one lighter than the other. It would not be physically possible for a man to throw two missiles with a range of less than 30m whilst he ran charging towards the enemy. This was especially true if that enemy was in turn charging towards him. Nor was it possible for a soldier to hold the second *pilum* with his left hand and still employ his shield properly. Not only was the Roman *scutum* very heavy, but it was held with a horizontal handgrip making it impractical to clutch this firmly and hold onto the shaft of a *pilum* at the same time. If both *pila* were carried in battle, which seems likely but is not certain, then the Romans must have halted for a while, close to the enemy line, to allow time to throw these before actually charging home. Probably a degree of hesitation a short distance apart was normal if both sides had failed to frighten the enemy sufficiently with their appearance, noise and confidence as they advanced. A recent study of the tactics of Roman infantry in the Republic suggests that exchanges of missiles could occupy considerable time.[35]

As the Roman centre started to come within missile range men on either side began to throw spears, javelins or *pila*. At first most probably dropped short or lacked the momentum to drive through the wooden shields which protected most of a man's body. Later, as the distance separating the two lines narrowed, some of the missiles began to strike home with greater force, punching through shields and perhaps even helmet or armour. Men crouched behind their long shields to gain as much coverage as possible, the Romans doubtless walking forward with heads bowed as if walking into a wind in the timeless posture of infantry advancing under fire. The majority of wounds were probably to the unprotected lower legs and occasionally to the face. Such casualties were probably led away to the rear, although there is some evidence of men fighting on with a number of non-incapacitating wounds in certain circumstances. The Roman *pilum* frequently had a barbed head and was designed to be very difficult to remove once it had punctured a shield. Some of the Gauls and Spaniards were most likely faced with the choice of dropping their shields after a *pilum* hit or fighting on with the shield awkwardly weighed down by the heavy weapon.

The whole Roman line appears to have halted once it came close to the enemy centre, even though much of the Roman front was still a fair distance from Hannibal's refused flanks. Close contact with the enemy often appears to have resulted in such inertia in ancient battles and the movements of armies were far more tentative than we might expect. In the central sector huge numbers of missiles were thrown by either side, but the vast majority fell short or struck harmlessly against shields. On either side only the front, and to a lesser extent the second ranks could actually see the enemy and make any effort to aim. The men behind were simply lobbing their weapons blindly forward in the hope that they would land somewhere amongst the enemy mass. There were roughly the same number of Gauls and Spaniards as there were *hastati* in the first Roman line and it is probable that both were formed in considerable depth. As a result many men, perhaps over half of each line, were too far away to have any hope of reaching the enemy with a thrown javelin. Fatal casualties were few on either side, but the sheer number of long-shafted javelins whizzing through the air made all the participants vividly aware that they were now in physical danger. This added to the pressure already created by the closeness of the enemy, their appearance of strength and confidence and the noise of war cries and trumpets, all of which continued throughout the exchange of missiles.

The Charge to Contact

As in the initial advance, neither side gained a decisive advantage in the missile battle and eventually the two lines met. Perhaps this was gradual, the Romans edging forward whilst throwing their *pila*, or more sudden as their officers were able to lead them in a charge sword in hand. The *hastati* had lost some of their order during the advance and subsequent javelin combat, but it still may have been possible, in spite of the noise and confusion, for centurions and tribunes to urge the maniples closest to the enemy to charge together. The Celts and Spaniards may have came forward to meet them, for it seems to have been unusual for infantry to remain entirely on the defensive against other foot, unless they were formed in an especially dense formation which made movement difficult. Shouting was redoubled as each side tried to appear as confident and frightening as possible when they at last closed.

Hand-to-hand combat is especially difficult for us to visualize accurately and all too often conjures up images which have more to do with Hollywood than with reality. In cinematic epics the two armies rapidly intermingle, every soldier fighting aggressively in combats which always end in the death of one of the participants. The whole swirling scene rarely lasts for more than a few frenzied minutes in which huge casualties are inflicted on both sides. In recent centuries hand-to-hand combat has been very rare, even in battles involving armies armed primarily with edged weapons, and massed fighting between formed units of men has been virtually unknown, since almost invariably one side or the other fled before actual contact. There is a good deal of evidence to suggest that in ancient battles it was also not uncommon for one side to rout before a blow had actually been struck or after very little fighting, but it is also certain that sometimes the opposing sides fought longer combats. From the descriptions in our sources, skeletal remains of the dead from battles fought with edged weapons, and comparison with modern studies of the behaviour of soldiers during the stress of combat, it is possible to reconstruct a picture of how such combats were fought. The evidence from more recent periods suggests that only a minority of soldiers even in élite units actually fought with the intention of killing the enemy. Another, probably smaller minority invariably failed to cope with combat, whilst the majority fought in a limited way, their priority to defend themselves far stronger than the urge to wound the enemy. As a result hand-to-hand combat between massed units was probably a good deal more tentative than our imagination or Hollywood images might suggest.[36]

The charge across the last few metres separating the two sides was accompanied by increased shouting and culminated in the noise of shield striking shield. Neither side needed to be moving very quickly to create the audible clash of arms described in some sources. It is extremely unlikely that men ran straight into each other hoping to barge into and knock their opponents over, for this risked losing their own balance and a man on the ground during a mêlée was immensely vulnerable. Nor did the men in the ranks behind push them on in such a physical sense as has been argued by many of the studies of hoplite warfare, since this in turn would only have unbalanced the front ranks. When the rear ranks of a formation pushed too closely behind the men in the lead it put these at a severe disadvantage, preventing them from fighting properly and causing heavy casualties as a result. Attackers began the charge at a run, but if the defenders stood or advanced as steadily to meet them, it seems that both lines checked their pace and then walked or shuffled into actual contact. They would only accelerate their running charge if the enemy gave way before them and it was a question of chasing and striking at their helpless backs.[37]

Attic helmet of a type common amongst the legions and alae at Cannae. The tubes on either side – one is missing as are the cheek pieces – held tall feather plumes intended to make the wearer look taller.

When the two lines met, the battle became in many respects a series of small duels fought between the individuals facing each other in the opposing front ranks. All of the soldiers engaged at this stage of the fighting at Cannae were primarily swordsmen and only men in the front rank were capable of reaching the enemy with their weapons. Both the Romans and the Spanish used swords with comparatively short blades which could be used to deliver either a cut or a thrust effectively. Many of the Gauls employed a longer type which was primarily intended for cutting. Some of these blades lacked a point altogether and many lacked any significant counterweight, such as a heavy pommel, so that they were unbalanced and end-heavy.

This added to the force of a blow, especially a downward slash, but made the sword awkward to wield. The natural first blow for a right-handed man using such a long sword was a downward, diagonal cut to the right side of his opponent's head or shoulders. After the sword had been raised again, it would then have been easier to aim a series of straighter slashes down at the enemy's left side. A warrior fighting in this way inevitably exposed his right arm and some of his right side as he did so. The shorter swords used by the Romans and Spanish could be used in a similar way to deliver downward cuts, although they had less reach and weight than the Gallic long sword, but were also effective as thrusting weapons. Ancient swordsmen stood in the opposite way to a modern fencer, with their right arm furthest from their opponent, since it was vital to have their shielded left side protecting against any threat. As a result, a man could not put the weight of his own body behind a lunge without turning his less well defended right side towards his opponent. Normal thrusts, delivered with no more than the strength and force of his right arm, were unlikely to penetrate an opponent's shield with sufficient force to carry on and inflict a wound. It was therefore necessary to aim blows around the enemy's shield, striking perhaps at his head or face, right arm or lower legs.

The Etrusco-Corinthian helmet was another type commonly used in this period. It was a derivative of the Corinthian helmet much used by Greek hoplites and had added cheek pieces to give some protection to the face.

A Roman legionary stood with his left foot forward and slightly crouched in the normal fighting position. From the front he was protected by his long, plywood shield which covered his body, left arm and upper legs. Additional protection for his torso came from a mail cuirass or metallic pectoral. His head was the most vital area not covered by the shield and this was why the helmet was the next most important piece of defensive equipment after the shield. The various patterns of bronze helmet in use by the Romans and their allies at this time offered good protection from a blow on the top of the head and, if provided with cheek pieces, a limited degree of coverage for the face. His left leg, the one nearest the enemy and as a result vulnerable, was often fitted with a metal greave. As far as we can tell most of the Spanish and Gallic warriors at Cannae lacked both helmets and body armour. In tribal warfare such expensive equipment tended to be the preserve of chieftains and the wealthy who were always a small minority, although it should be remembered that these well equipped men would tend to take their place in the front rank of a formation. We do not know whether many of these men wore captured Roman armour or whether Hannibal had reserved this exclusively for his Libyans. Most warriors relied exclusively on their long, flat shields for protection, making it all the more devastating a loss if a shield had been lost to a Roman *pilum*.

La Tène Celtic sword. Long bladed slashing swords much like this example were carried by many of the Gallic warriors fighting for Hannibal at Cannae. These weapons were end heavy, adding to the force of a downward blow, but also making them awkward to wield.

It was very difficult to disable an opponent with a single blow; either a heavy strike to the head, a massive thrust past shield and through any armour to the body, or a hit on the leg breaking the bone and causing the victim to fall. Attempting to deliver such a strong cut or thrust exposed the attacker to greater risk of wounding, especially as his right arm, and perhaps part of his right side, lost the protection of his shield. It was less risky to deliver weaker attacks to the unprotected extremities of an opponent, even though this was unlikely to kill him quickly. There is some skeletal evidence from battlefield graves in the ancient period, and rather more from the middle age. The pattern and type of wounds is remarkably consistent and suggests how hand-to-hand combats were fought. (However, it is important to remember that only wounds which involved damage to bone are preserved in this record. Injuries to fleshy parts of the body or the stomach would not leave any trace. Bearing

in mind that our information is derived from battlefield grave finds, we have no record of the men who suffered wounds but survived the battle.) The sheer physical force of some blows surprised many specialists, but such single, almost certainly fatal, injuries were rare. Usually the dead suffered a number of lesser wounds, none of which were incapacitating, before being finished off by a heavier blow to the head. The most common were hits to the lower legs, especially the left leg nearest the enemy, the right arm, undefended by a shield, and the left side of the head. Even a number of such light wounds did not seriously impair the man's ability to continue fighting.

We should imagine the two front ranks separated by a metre or so, prodding and cutting at each other in a constant clatter of blade against shield, helmet and sometimes flesh. Once again individuals hoped that their appearance – physical size, expression, plumes, shiny armour, impressive hair or beard – and the noise they made would intimidate their opponents and aid their victory. Cato the Elder, who served during the Second Punic War as a cavalryman and junior officer, although he probably was not at Cannae, always maintained that a soldier's bearing, confidence and the ferociousness of his war cry were more important that his actual skill with a blade. The majority of men took care to shelter as much as possible behind their shields, warding off blows and occasionally delivering a careful attack themselves. Such men inflicted only minor wounds, weakening an opponent but not putting him out of the fight.

A minority of soldiers fought with far more aggression, aiming savage cuts or thrusts at the enemy, and it was these who inflicted nearly all of the serious

injuries, although they in turn suffered a higher proportion of casualties. Some men, especially amongst the Romans, may have used their heavy shields to buffet and unbalance the enemy, punching with their whole weight behind the boss. Ideally, when a man in the opposing front rank was killed or knocked to the ground, the victor stepped into his place. This was highly dangerous for he risked attack from the men to the front and sides in the second rank of the enemy formation, but it was also the best way to begin the enemy's rout. As soldiers began to feel that they were no longer protected on their flanks by their comrades and that enemies

The Montefortino helmet was probably the most common type of headgear used by the legions in this period, and remained in service for several centuries. Based originally on a Gallic design, and so quite possibly also in use amongst Hannibal's Celts, it had a high bowl which offered good protection against downward cuts.

were amongst them, their nervousness could quickly turn to panic. It was at this stage in the fighting, when a unit turned and fled, that most casualties occurred, and this was the single most important factor in explaining the far higher casualties always suffered by the losing side in an ancient battle. Men in flight lost the vital protection of their shields and the victors were able to strike freely at their backs. The sight of enemies, who until recently had posed a direct threat to them, turning their backs seems to have encouraged the majority of soldiers, the ones who fought with the intention of staying alive, to act aggressively and expunge their fears in a one-sided massacre of all they could catch. Minor wounds, most of all wounds to the legs, suffered during the fighting could now prove fatal, for the weakened men were often slower to run and more likely to be caught and finished off by the vengeful pursuers. Blows delivered when the victim was helpless were stronger and more closely spaced. It appears that it was not uncommon for the attackers to strike repeatedly at the fallen enemy, so that as many as seven or eight massive cuts were delivered to the skull, any one of which would probably have proved fatal (see illustration on page 158). The savagery of such attacks on already defeated enemies is a powerful reminder that battles, especially hand-to-hand battles, are not fought by calm soldiers fighting coldly, carefully and logically, but by frightened, vulnerable and emotional human beings.[38]

This was the most dramatic end to a hand-to-hand encounter, when men from one unit cut their way into the enemy ranks, created a panic and inflicted a brief massacre as the defeated group turned to flee, but it was not the most common outcome of a fight. More often in the initial clash neither side was able to gain such a decisive advantage and if any men tried to break the enemy ranks they were swiftly killed themselves. The very fact that both sides had sufficient confidence to meet in hand-to-hand fighting in the first place, rather than being persuaded to retire or flee by the enemy's intimidating advance and the volleys of missiles, which they had hurled, made it unlikely that either would swiftly give way. Hand-to-hand fighting was physically strenuous and emotionally draining. If one side did not quickly collapse then the actual combat could not continue for more than a few minutes. Instead the two sides seem to have drawn apart, perhaps little more than a few metres, for even at such a short distance they were out of the reach of the enemy's hand-held weapons. There they drew breath, shouted at the enemy and, perhaps, threw any remaining missiles at them.

After each such lull, one side or the other would surge forward into contact again and another brief flurry of actual hand-to-hand fighting occur. If no outside force intervened, then victory would eventually go to the side which endured the stress of staying so close to the enemy for the longest and was still able to urge enough of its men forward to renew the fighting. The pauses in the fighting most probably grew longer and longer as it became more diffi-cult to persuade the weary soldiers to advance and fight another time and another. The great emphasis the Romans placed on encouraging and rewarding individual boldness in their soldiers acknowledged the very real need for aggressive soldiers who would lead a fresh charge forward and try to fight their way into the enemy's formation. These situations also made great demands on an army's officers to lead the way, even though this might mean that they suffered casualties at a disproportionately high rate. The Romans had an *optio* behind each century to hold the men in place and a centurion in the front rank to urge them onwards. Centurions were supposed to be selected for their determination and skill as leaders rather than individual prowess in fighting, and as infantry combats drew on this sort of stubbornness was especially important. There were six tribunes per legion and the majority of these appear to have fought with the heavy infantry in battle. They were not tied to any one position, but moved around the battle line, encouraging the men and committing reserves as necessary. In addition to these men there were senior officers. Servilius Geminus began the battle with the infantry and he was subsequently joined there by Paullus, who is described as moving to crisis points in the line, leading local charges and fighting hand to hand, and always urging on his soldiers to greater effort. The Roman army at Cannae had an especially large number of senior officers concentrated on a limited frontage to inspire the men and control the battle. Hannibal's decision to advance the middle of his line and provoke a battle first in the very centre acted to reduce even more the width of the initial contact and so concentrate the attentions of so many officers in this limited area. On the Carthaginian side, both Hannibal himself and his brother Mago acted in a similar fashion to the Roman officers, keeping close to the fighting to inspire and direct their men, and there were presumably many junior officers and tribal chieftains performing the same task.[39]

The third phase of the battle. Hasdrubal rallies his men from the pursuit of the Roman cavalry and reforms his squadrons. The Numidians continue to skirmish with Varro's Italian cavalry. In the centre, the pressure of the Roman advance has started to force back the Gauls and Spaniards. Their most advanced units have now been pushed back level with the main line.

Early in the fighting it might have been possible to persuade the entire line to advance together, but this sort of order was swiftly lost in the chaos of noise, dust and confusion. As the struggle went on it is likely that it was hard to persuade more than an individual maniple or company to surge forward and renew the fight at the same time, and eventually things may have degenerated further so that only small groups managed to act together. Close contact with the enemy caused unit formations to degenerate into loose masses, and we should never imagine combats as fought by neat blocks of men, the

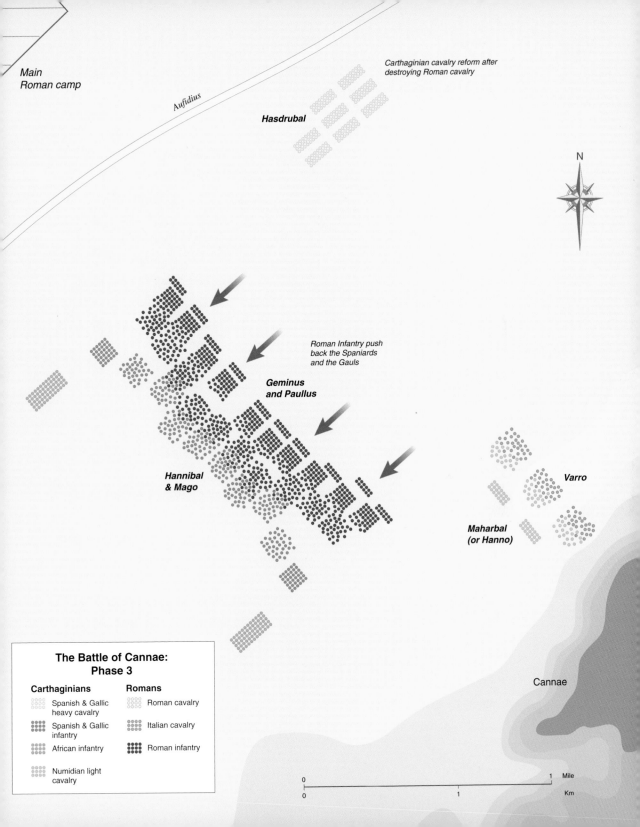

Main
Roman camp

Aufidius

Hasdrubal

*Carthaginian cavalry reform after
destroying Roman cavalry*

N

*Roman Infantry push
back the Spaniards
and the Gauls*

**Geminus
and Paullus**

**Hannibal
& Mago**

Varro

**Maharbal
(or Hanno)**

Cannae

The Battle of Cannae:
Phase 3

Carthaginians   **Romans**

Spanish & Gallic   Roman cavalry
heavy cavalry

Spanish & Gallic   Italian cavalry
infantry

African infantry   Roman infantry

Numidian light
cavalry

0   1   Mile

0   1   Km

soldiers in perfect rank and file. Under the pressure of combat the less enthusiastic soldiers tried to escape, edging to the rear, whilst the boldest pressed
forward. The majority massed in the middle, ready to follow the bold few if
their attack proved successful or the more nervous if these started to flee. The
fighting line was not a solid wall of men, but a row of increasingly rough
groups clustered together, each man's position a reflection of his keenness. Its
openness allowed officers to move around with some freedom, only occasionally actually fighting hand-to-hand themselves, although they were
always at risk of being hit by missiles or singled out by a lone attacker. Facing
this was another similar line formed by the enemy, the two usually separated
by a short distance, save where a unit or group had managed to build up sufficient aggression to charge into contact. It was difficult for most soldiers to
know how well even their own unit's fight was going unless they were in the
front rank, and only if they could make sense of the overwhelming noise could
they possibly gauge the progress of the fight elsewhere in the line. This created
a permanent state of nervousness, since men knew that, if a serious breakthrough occurred in their line and it collapsed into flight, then the men most
likely to be killed by the pursuing enemy were the ones who hesitated before
they ran.

Once again, our sources are vague as to how long the fighting continued
after the Romans had reached the advanced centre of the Punic line, but both
Polybius and Livy testified to the stiff resistance put up by the Gallic and
Spanish infantry to the Roman juggernaut. Here, as at Telamon and some
other battles, the tribal warriors belied the literary stereotype of the wild
barbarian whose initial ferocity rapidly declined as he grew weary. In numbers
the Punic centre was roughly equal to the Roman *hastati* and, since they occupied a similar frontage, was presumably deployed in much the same depth.
Depth gave a formation great resilience in combat and this, along with the
presence of so many senior officers, encouraging the men and sharing with
them the risks of combat, prolonged the fight. Livy tells us that, ' ... at first
equally matched in strength and confidence, the Gauls and Spaniards stood

firm for as long as their formation held. At length the Romans, surging forward again and again on an even front and in dense array drove back the advanced wedge [curved line] formed by the enemy which was too thin and weak to hold.'[40]

The Gauls and Spaniards had no immediate supports, whilst the *hastati* were just the first of the three Roman lines. The manipular system was intended to allow the reinforcement of the fighting line with fresh troops, with the intention that their enthusiasm would persuade the whole line to surge forward into contact against the weary enemy. The reserve lines could reinforce the fighting line if it was coming under pressure, or advance to exploit any successes and breakthroughs it managed to achieve. The many senior officers, tribunes, prefects and above, who had pressed forward to oversee the fighting in the centre of the line were there not just to inspire the men and witness their behaviour, but also to control the commitment of the second and third lines. However well the Punic infantry fought, in the end, the Romans' weight of numbers would come to bear as more and more maniples were fed into the combat. Eventually the pressure grew too great and the Celts and Spaniards began to give way. They did so slowly at first, perhaps moving back after each flurry of fighting, but still facing the enemy. We read in accounts of other battles of the ancient world of lines which were forced back several hundred metres or even more than a kilometre, but still maintained a front and did not dissolve into rout. At Cannae the Punic centre at first gave way gradually in this fashion, but, as the Romans poured more and more men into the main line to exploit this success, the line broke and ran. As usual, the Carthaginian foot seem to have suffered very heavy casualties as they fled from a vengeful enemy.[41]

Encirclement

As Hannibal's centre collapsed and the legionaries chased sword in hand after the fleeing warriors, the Roman plan appeared to be working. Varro was still on the left flank, his allied horsemen engaged in sporadic and indecisive

skirmishing with the elusive Numidian cavalry. The lack of movement on this wing was entirely satisfactory from the consul's point of view, for his task was simply to protect the flanks of the heavy infantry and allow them to win the great victory. It is questionable to what extent Varro could have observed the progress of the fighting in the centre for the dust would only have added to the confusion, and most unlikely that he knew of the flight of the Roman cavalry on the right, but he may well have been able to see that the Roman foot were steadily pressing forward. Paullus, Servilius and the other officers with the infantry knew that the plan was working and redoubled their efforts to pour more of their reserves into the gap, giving the enemy no opportunity to rally. In the centre of the battlefield a great mass of Roman infantrymen some tens of thousands strong pressed forward to complete the rout of the enemy foot.

Massed battles presented many problems to sculptors and artists. This scene from the early second century AD shows a battle from the Emperor Trajan's Dacian Wars. The uniforms of the Roman soldiers at Cannae were very different.

The Roman legion was supposed to operate with wide gaps between its maniples and significant intervals between each of the three lines. The openness of its formation allowed the legion to advance without falling into disorder even over comparatively rough terrain. It is impossible, even for well drilled troops, to march in a perfectly straight line, and the more uneven the terrain, the more probable that a unit will veer to one side or the other. The wide intervals between the maniples of the legion allowed them to cope with such deviation without units colliding and merging together and ceasing to be independent tactical entities. The unusual formation adopted by the Roman infantry at Cannae sacrificed this openness and with it most of the flexibility of the manipular system. Varro deployed the maniples on a very narrow frontage but in great depth and reduced the width of the gaps between each unit. As soon as the Roman line began to move forward, these intervals would have tended to disappear, the maniples merging together so that instead of many semi-independent tactical units there was simply one mass. The greater depth of each maniple may have reduced the space normally maintained between each of the three lines, but,

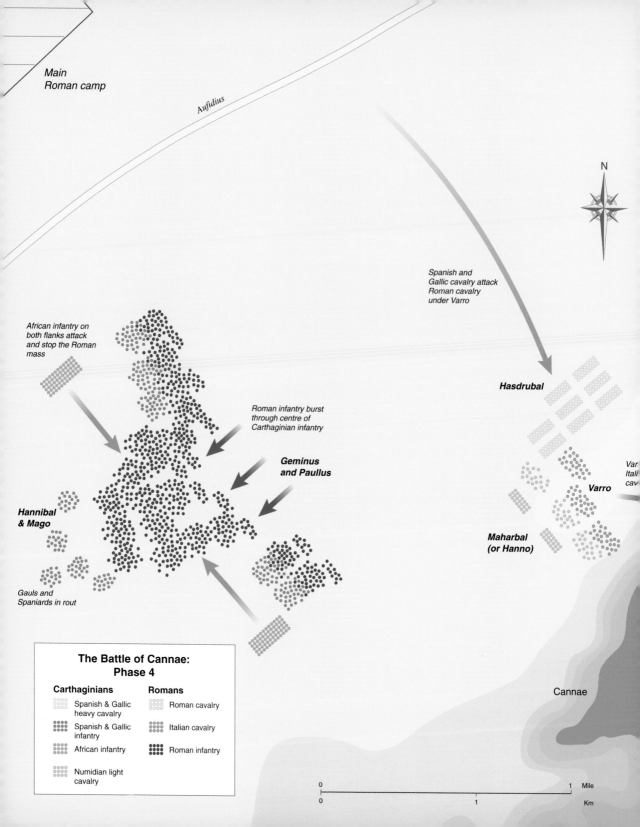

Main
Roman camp

Aufidius

N

Spanish and
Gallic cavalry attack
Roman cavalry
under Varro

*African infantry on
both flanks attack
and stop the Roman
mass*

Hasdrubal

*Roman infantry burst
through centre of
Carthaginian infantry*

**Geminus
and Paullus**

Var
Itali
cav

Varro

**Hannibal
& Mago**

**Maharbal
(or Hanno)**

*Gauls and
Spaniards in rout*

The Battle of Cannae:
Phase 4

Carthaginians	Romans
Spanish & Gallic heavy cavalry	Roman cavalry
Spanish & Gallic infantry	Italian cavalry
African infantry	Roman infantry
Numidian light cavalry	

Cannae

0   1   Mile

0   1   Km

even if it had not, the confined nature of the plain between the Aufidius and the hills around Cannae probably had the same result. There may well have been some blurring between the lines as well as amongst the individual maniples as the Roman centre lumbered forward.

The Roman plan relied entirely upon their numerically superior infantry to win the day. The cavalry were there primarily to hold off Hannibal's better quality and more numerous horsemen for long enough to allow the Roman foot to break the Punic line. It was therefore important for the legions to win as quickly as possible. The Roman officers who clustered just behind the fighting line knew this, and were all the more willing to feed men from the reserve lines into the combat. Hannibal had deliberately placed his centre much closer to the enemy than his flanks and, as he hoped, it was there that the infantry fighting first developed. As the Romans began to make headway against this advanced position, more and more men from the reserve lines were sent to reinforce their fighting line. It was not just the maniples directly behind the engaged units which were drawn into the struggle, for Polybius tells us that large numbers of men on either side were sucked into the combat. The distinction between separate maniples had already started to dissolve as the army advanced, and especially amongst the units who then came into contact with the enemy, but rapidly vanished altogether as more and more men were packed into the combat being fought on a very small front. The Romans' breakthrough was achieved at the price of their good order and their infantry were now more like a crowd than an organized body divided into distinct sub-units closely controlled by their officers.[42]

The fourth phase of the battle. As the Romans pour more and more reserves into the fighting, the pressure of their numbers breaks through the Punic line. The Gallic and Spanish warbands in the centre break and stream to the rear. Scenting victory, the Romans pursue. By now their units have lost much of their order and the three neat lines in which they began the battle are only a memory. In the meantime Hasdrubal leads his cavalry against the rear of Varro's Italians. The latter panic and flee before a blow has been struck.

Yet victory must have seemed close as the Roman mass punched straight through the very centre of Hannibal's line. The Celts and Spaniards on either side of the gaping hole in their line seem not to have broken, but retreated in better order. The concentration of the overwhelming weight of the Roman attack on the centre and the use of most reserves there probably meant that they were under far less pressure. The Romans surged forward until they were level with the starting position of the flanks of Hannibal's main line and kept going, for there was nothing to oppose them. The attack still had considerable momentum, but very little order, and was no longer under anyone's control. In such a mass an officer of any rank could only influence the men immediately around him.

As the Roman mass streamed forward, they found themselves with Hannibal's Libyan infantry arrayed in columns on either side of them. The Libyans had as yet played no part in the fighting and were fresh and in good order. There were probably no more than 8,000–10,000 of them, divided into two forces each roughly the size of a Roman legion. The similarity went further, since they were now dressed and armed with Roman equipment stripped from the dead of Trebia and Trasimene, although it is unlikely that they had adopted manipular organization and tactics and probable that they still fought as a phalanx. We do not know who gave the orders – perhaps Hannibal had ridden from his routed centre and gone in person to one of the Libyan columns, sent a messenger, or simply explained in detail to the Libyans' commanders before the battle what was required of them – but the column on the left turned to form a line facing to the right and those on the right turned to face left. Then the two phalanxes marched forward and attacked into the flanks of the crowded mass of pursuing Roman soldiers.[43]

The Romans were in no position to form fighting lines to face either of the new threats. The maniples were hopelessly intermingled and beyond the control of their leaders. The already confused situation was probably exacerbated by the Roman-like appearance of the bodies of infantry moving towards them and it may have taken some time to realize that these were hostile. The loss of a clear sense of direction seems to be common under the stress of combat and few men may have realized that there should not be any friendly troops approaching from that direction. Small groups of soldiers may have turned to form rough lines facing the enemy, but they lacked missile weapons, were fatigued through combat and never formed a coherent line. The Libyan's charge stopped the Roman advance dead, robbing it of all momentum. There were now no organized reserves in the Roman army to feed into the combat and renew the surge forward. Officers improvised as best they could, but movement in the packed ranks was probably difficult and became even harder as it contracted under the pressure of the twin enemy attacks. The two phalanxes of Libyans gripped the Romans like a vice, and around them the surviving Celtic and Spanish troops, joined perhaps after a while by some of the routers, pressed round to add to the fighting line. The Romans were now fighting on three sides, but unable to support the combat in any direction properly.

In the meantime events had occurred elsewhere on the battlefield which would seal the fate of the Roman centre. Hasdrubal had led his close order cavalry in a devastatingly brutal charge against the Roman right wing, shattering and virtually destroying it in a brief pursuit. The Carthaginian had kept his men under tight control and, when they had rested and reformed, he led them behind the Roman main line, moving against Varro on the left, and ignoring the massed infantry in the enemy centre. Varro's allied horsemen were still engaged in their stand-off with the Numidians, but the sight of the lines of Hasdrubal's Gauls and Spaniards approaching from the rear utterly shattered their spirit. Without waiting for the Carthaginians to charge home, the Roman left wing dissolved into a panicked flight in which the consul joined. Their position was untenable, and, if they had in fact formed with their flank on the hills around Cannae, any delay in flight might have resulted in their being trapped. They could not have won any combat with a more numerous enemy attacking from two sides, but their flight sealed the fate of the Roman army. Hasdrubal had once again kept his men closely in hand, helped perhaps by the enemy's swift flight, which meant that the Punic horse did not have to go through with their charge and fight a mêlée. He gave orders for the Numidians to pursue the fleeing enemy horsemen – a task to which they were ideally suited – and led his own command against the rear of the Roman foot. The confused mass of 50,000 or so Roman and allied heavy infantryman and maybe as many as 20,000 *velites* was now surrounded.[44]

Annihilation

There is a tendency for descriptions of the battle to stop at this point, when Hannibal's tactical genius had allowed his army to surround the more numerous Romans by using the weight of the enemy's attack against them. Viewed at the grand tactical level, all the significant moves in the battle had already occurred and the utter defeat of the Roman army was now inevitable. There was to be little tactical sophistication in the final phase of the battle, but fighting would continue for much of the rest of the day as the Carthaginians attacked from all sides and systematically slaughtered the greater part of the Roman infantry mass.[45]

The fifth phase of the battle. The Numidians are sent in pursuit of the fleeing enemy, whilst Hasdrubal's close order cavalry again reform. In the centre the Romans have degenerated into little more than a crowd. Suddenly attacked on each flank by a fresh body of Libyans, the momentum of their advance is lost. Gradually the Gauls and Spaniards reform, closing around the mass of the enemy. The fate of the Romans is sealed when Hasdrubal launches a series of charges against their rear.

The reduction in size of the gaps normally maintained between the maniples and lines in a Roman army caused units to merge together into one crowd as the army had advanced, especially when more and more troops were drawn into the very centre of the line. Probably the narrowness of the plain between Cannae and the River Aufidius, originally attractive to Varro because it offered protection for his flanks, speeded the disintegration of the Romans' order. By the time that the breakthrough in the centre had been stopped in its tracks by the Libyans' counter-attack and Hasdrubal's cavalry swept down against the Roman rear, there were no longer ordered maniples and lines of Roman and allied infantry, but a disorganized mass. There was, for instance, no question of a reserve line of *triarii* simply turning round, kneeling behind their shields and presenting an impenetrable line of spear points at the attacking cavalry. This has sometimes mistakenly been taken to suggest that the entire *triarii* were absent, probably guarding the larger camp, otherwise Hasdrubal's men could not have

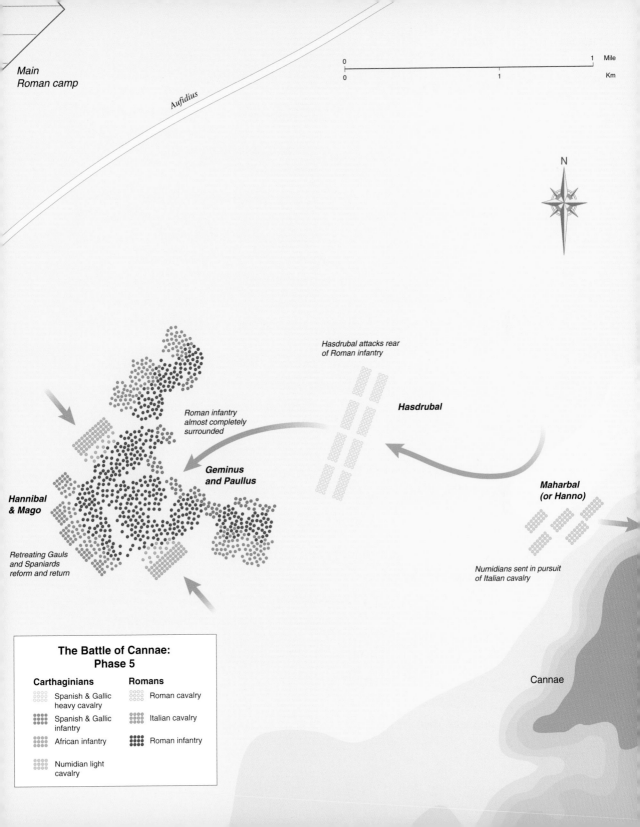

Main
Roman camp

Aufidius

0   1   Mile
0   1   Km

N

Hasdrubal attacks rear
of Roman infantry

Hasdrubal

Roman infantry
almost completely
surrounded

**Geminus
and Paullus**

**Maharbal
(or Hanno)**

**Hannibal
& Mago**

Retreating Gauls
and Spaniards
reform and return

Numidians sent in pursuit
of Italian cavalry

Cannae

The Battle of Cannae:
Phase 5

Carthaginians   **Romans**

Spanish & Gallic   Roman cavalry
heavy cavalry

Spanish & Gallic   Italian cavalry
infantry

African infantry   Roman infantry

Numidian light
cavalry

acted so effectively against the Roman rear. However, this fails to appreciate the confusion amongst the legionaries and allies by this stage of the battle. In places some groups, perhaps occasionally even whole maniples, of these veteran spearmen may have been able to form a dense knot with weapons towards the enemy, but there was no question of an entire third line facing to the rear. Most of the army's officers had been drawn forward to assist in and direct the fighting in the centre, and there was certainly no one left in charge of the entire third line, which anyway is unlikely still to have existed as a clearly distinct entity. Hasdrubal's cavalrymen could not have charged home against any group of infantry which remained in close formation facing towards them. Instead, such knots of men were bombarded with missiles and the cavalry swept on to charge wherever the Roman foot were scattered and unprepared.[46]

The Roman foot were hemmed in on all sides and nowhere able to form a coherent and properly supported fighting line. Time after time the Libyans, and however many of the Gauls and Spaniards had rallied, renewed their attack, surging forward into actual contact to fight a brief mêlée. They fought till they were weary and the edges of their swords and spear points blunted through killing. As the fight drew on, the lulls between each bout of actual combat can only have grown longer and longer as it became harder for their officers to urge the exhausted men forward once again. Hannibal, Mago, Hasdrubal and other officers continued to stay close to the fighting, inspiring their men, trying to organize the fight as far as this was possible and occasionally leading them personally in a charge. In the same way Paullus, Servilius, and the military tribunes still moved around amongst the Roman mass, trying to bring aid and encouragement to some of the many crisis points.

The Romans' position was hopeless. They were even more tired than the enemy, especially the Libyans who had remained in reserve in the early phases of the battle, and the disintegration of their formation and unit structure hindered their efforts to fight. Hand-to-hand fighting with edged weapons required massive physical effort. Hannibal's professional soldiers were probably fitter and better trained to cope with this. Although the bulk of the Roman army came from peasant stock, accustomed to prolonged physical labour, if not to the noise and confusion of battle, the massive expansion of the army before Cannae may have swept into its ranks many younger, older or less fit soldiers. Even so many seem to have put up a very determined resistance and Hannibal's victory was only to be bought at a high price. The Romans admired stubbornness and expected it of their ordinary soldiers. Many of the men can have known little of what was going on in the rest of the battlefield and perhaps did not realize that the entire army faced disaster. Some fought on, as the legionaries had in the equally hopeless situation at Trasimene.[47]

As the day drew on, the hot wind blowing clouds of dust across the dry plain, Hannibal's infantry closed again and again to fight hand to hand with the Romans. Wearily they cut and jabbed at the legionaries sheltering behind their shields, trying to break into their ranks. Sometimes they failed to make any impression and the two sides drew apart after a brief time of actual combat. Very occasionally, the Romans forced them back locally, killing any men who tried to hack their way into the Roman ranks. Most often it was the Roman line which went back slowly, facing the enemy, or dissolved into rout. Then the Carthaginians pursued them, striking at unprotected backs, killing especially the men wounded in the earlier fighting who were now too weak or slow to escape. Knocked to the ground, they were dispatched with frenzied blows, usually to the head. Sometimes the press in the Roman ranks was so great that they could not retreat even when things went badly for them in the combat. Unable to escape because of the mass of men behind them, legionaries were cut down offering little resistance. Some, inside the formation and unable to see what was going on, may have had little opportunity to realize their peril until the men in front were cut down and enemies suddenly appeared to strike at them. Still the Carthaginians continued to press on, their shields and the breasts of their horses stained with blood.[48]

In the end widespread Roman resistance collapsed as the army broke and fled. Most men were cut down as they ran, but significant numbers seem to have escaped to the temporary safety of the two Roman camps or the surrounding villages. Although the Carthaginians were attacking from all sides, they do not appear to have formed a complete ring. This was probably especially true of the cavalry, who had to remain mobile if they were to be most effective. Nor do we know how many of Hannibal's other foot were rallied or had remained in reasonable shape to support the Libyans, and it is more than possible that, until the very end, the Punic army remained significantly outnumbered. Polybius tells us only that Paullus eventually succumbed to his many wounds received whilst fighting heroically and leading the stiffest Roman resistance. Livy's version is much more detailed and rich in pathos. He claimed that a military tribune, one Cnaeus Lentulus, discovered the badly wounded Paullus propped up against a rock. Lentulus offered him his horse, but Paullus nobly refused and then the two were swept apart by a group of fleeing Romans, closely pursued by the enemy. Lentulus was saved by the speed of his horse, whilst the consul died under a hail of enemy missiles, the Carthaginians passing him without realizing whom they had just killed. The scene provided Livy, and those other later authors who followed the same tradition, to give Paullus another speech making it clear that he was not responsible for the disaster and still adhered to Fabius' cautious strategy. It is interesting that this account implies a fluid, mass flight of the Roman army rather than a fight to the death. Most probably the story is yet another invention intended to salvage Paullus' reputation and lay the blame for the disaster on his colleague. There was in fact no obligation for a Roman commander to die when his army suffered defeat, and the suicide of defeated leaders only ever became common during Rome's later civil wars. However, the scandals of Paullus' first consulship may well have made him far more concerned about his reputation and unwilling to endure more controversy.[49]

Livy says that 7,000 fugitives made it to the smaller Roman camp and 10,000 to the larger camp on the far bank of the river, although these may well be the troops left behind as garrison there by Paullus. The greater part of the Roman army now lay dead or dying on the plain beside the Aufidius, but, as is so often the case, there is disagreement in our sources about their numbers. Polybius says that around 70,000 Romans fell in the battle, a further 10,000 were captured soon afterwards in the larger camp, and only around 10,000 foot and 370 horse managed to escape. There is clearly a problem with these figures, for they amount to a total of over 90,000, which is larger than the figure he gives for the entire Roman strength before the battle. Livy's figures are 45,500 infantry and 2,700 cavalry killed and 3,000 and 1,500, respectively, captured immediately; these seem more plausible and conform roughly with the rounded up figure of 50,000 repeated on several occasions both in his account and those of other authors. More than half of the Roman army had fallen, but the cost of achieving this slaughter was dear for Hannibal's army. Polybius states that the Punic losses amounted to 4,000 Gauls, 1,500 Spaniards and Libyans, and 200 cavalry, a total of 5,700. Livy provides the higher estimate of about 8,000 men. In either case this was an appallingly high figure for a victorious army, representing a casualty rate of 11.5 per cent or 16 per cent respectively. This was more than two to three times the average loss suffered by winning armies in the battles of the ancient world and testifies to the harshness of the fighting even after the Romans were surrounded. It is even possible that these figures included only the dead or mortally wounded, so that perhaps they should be at the very least doubled to include wounded. If so, then Hannibal's losses were staggering.[50]

Varro had escaped to the town of Venusia, but his colleague was dead and so were the proconsul Servilius Geminus, and Marcus Minucius Rufus, Fabius' *Magister Equitum*, by that time probably serving as a tribune. Both of the quaestors, Lucius Atilius and Lucius Furius Bibaculus, elected as financial officials and deputies for the consuls, had also fallen. Of the forty-eight military tribunes commanding the army's eight legions more than half, twenty-nine, were killed. In addition to these were eighty men either already members of the Senate or whose achievements justified their enrolment during the next census. Somewhere between a quarter and a third of Roman senators were killed or went into captivity at Cannae, and many more members had lost sons or other relations. The equestrians who provided the cavalry also suffered great losses, as did the yeoman farmers who provided the bulk of the legions' heavy infantry. Never had any defeat struck so hard at the very heart of Roman society. As night fell on 2 August 216 BC, Rome's very future seemed in doubt.

MOPPING UP

The plain beside the River Aufidius must have been a truly ghastly sight after the battle. Over 50,000 men lay dead or dying in an area of little more than a few square kilometres, many of the bodies horribly disfigured from blows with edged weapons. Many wounded survived to the next day, as the stench of blood and corruption grew worse in the sun's warmth. Whilst the Romans and Italians were dispatched by Punic soldiers, the Carthaginians received whatever medical care was offered by their comrades. Many of the Gallic warriors in the army were accompanied by their wives and families and we must imagine these women searching for their husbands amongst the heaps of bodies that night and the next morning. Other figures moved amongst the dead and dying to plunder anything of value. There is a

There is very little direct skeletal evidence for the battles of the Ancient World, but the few surviving battle-field graves show a very similar distribution of injuries to bones excavated from the sites of other battles fought predominantly with edged weapons. This skull found at the site of the Battle of Wisby, fought in Sweden in 1361, shows the kind of head injuries those at Cannae could have expected.

nightmarish quality about many of the descriptions of the aftermath of Cannae, Livy saying that the carnage was 'shocking even to enemies'. He describes the masses of bodies, infantry and cavalry intermingled, the wounded begging for death as an end to their suffering, and other men who had scraped holes in the ground and buried their heads to smother themselves. The Carthaginians are supposed to have found a live Numidian, 'his nose and ears ripped' where the Roman who had lain on top of him had bitten at his enemy with his dying breath. Later sources would invent further horrors, claiming that Hannibal bridged the River Aufidius with Roman corpses. The reality of Cannae was probably even more appalling than such horrific inventions, for it remains one of the bloodiest single day's fighting in history, rivalling the massed slaughter of the British Army on the first day of the Somme offensive in 1916.[1]

Cannae was a stunning blow to the Romans. The greatest army ever fielded by the Republic, which had marched so confidently into battle, had been almost annihilated. The survivors, clustered in the dubious sanctuary offered by the ramparts of the Roman camps, were mostly in shock, and only a few were capable of any effort to escape. The men in the larger camp had played little part in the battle, apart from an abortive attack on Hannibal's camp, and were presumably still in organized units and led by their officers. They are supposed to have sent a message to the other camp, instructing the men there to cross the river and join forces, so that both groups could then move to Canusium in the west. The nervous survivors in the smaller camp expressed little enthusiasm for this plan, but Livy tells us that one tribune, Publius Sempronius Tuditanus, managed to persuade 600 men to break out and cross the ford, brushing aside the few parties of Numidians – probably more interested in looting than fighting – who got in their way. According to another source, a mere sixty-two men followed Tuditanus and another tribune, Cnaeus Octavius. Joined by a part, but not all of the garrison of the larger camp, this force then escaped to Canusium, having to pass Hannibal's camp en route. From a later passage it appears that these numbered around 4,000 infantry and 200 cavalry.[2]

Polybius claims that Hannibal reduced the Roman camps on the evening of the 2 August and also rounded up several thousand fugitives who had taken shelter in the ruins of Cannae itself. In Livy's version it was not until the next day that Hannibal moved against the Roman encampments and this seems rather more likely, for his army can only have been utterly exhausted at the end of the battle. Roman resistance was feeble and the camps soon surrendered, giving up all their equipment and possessions apart from a single tunic per man, and agreeing to pay a ransom according to status. The terms of the surrender made it very clear that Hannibal's victory was overwhelming. About 12,800 men were taken into captivity from the two camps and 2,000 in Cannae itself to add to the 4,500 captured on the battlefield. As with the casualties, these were probably a half-and-half mix of Romans and allies, although it is just possible that some of the latter were more willing to surrender, aware that Hannibal had treated allied captives very favourably in the last two years.[3]

Varro had fled to Venusia in the west, but had only a small number of cavalrymen (seventy according to Polybius; fifty in Livy) with him. The largest group of Roman survivors was the one at Canusium, where they were given shelter by the inhabitants and then benefited from the largesse of a local woman named Busa who distributed food, clean clothing and money. Livy's account makes no more mention of Tuditanus, and, according to him, command devolved on four military tribunes, Quintus Fabius Maximus (the dictator's son and himself subsequently consul in 213), Lucius Bibulus, Publius Cornelius Scipio (son of the consul of 218 BC wounded at Ticinus), and Appius Claudius. Scipio and Claudius, although the youngest of the group – Scipio was still in his teens – assumed command through force of personality and their continued confidence. Panic threatened to break out when it was revealed that a group of young noblemen were planning to flee abroad, believing that the Republic was doomed. They were led by Marcus Caecilius Metellus, a member of a very distinguished family, and Publius Furius Philus, whose father had been consul with Flaminius in 223 BC. Scipio arrested Metellus and his followers and, sword in hand, made them join him in a solemn oath never to abandon the Republic or even permit others to speak of doing so.[4]

Slowly in the days that followed, more bedraggled fugitives came in to join the parties at Venusia and Cannae. Within a short time Varro had mustered another 4,500 men at Venusia, who were provided for generously by the population of the town. The tribunes at Canusium, hearing a report of the consul's survival and his rallying of this force, sent a messenger to request instructions. Rather than have them join him at Venusia, Varro himself shifted his command to Canusium, moving somewhat nearer the enemy in the process. Livy mentions that around 10,000 men were gathered in the town, but it is not clear whether this was before or after the consul and his forces arrived. Something resembling a field army was being reassembled and in the end two legions were formed from the survivors of Cannae. It was a pitiful remnant of the huge army which had begun the campaign, and far too weak to approach Hannibal.[5]

HOW TO USE A VICTORY

When the first news reached Rome of the catastrophe suffered by its army, the inhabitants did not yet know that even these few soldiers had survived. The State had placed unprecedented resources of men and material in the hands of the consuls to confront the enemy. Instead of the anticipated victory this had produced another defeat, far worse in scale even than Trebia or Trasimene, both of which had still shocked a population accustomed to victory. Panic gripped the city, people fearing both their own future and the fate of family members with the army. The depleted Senate met to debate their course of action, and it was Fabius Maximus who persuaded the senators to restrict public mourning and post guards at all the gates to prevent panicked flight. As importantly, scouts were sent out along the main roads to the south to seek any news of Hannibal. That was the vital question: what was the victorious enemy going to do now?[6]

Livy pictured the scene as Hannibal's officers rode across the battlefield after the fighting:

Clustered around Hannibal the rest congratulated him on his victory, and suggested that, since he had concluded so great a war, he should allow himself and his weary soldiers to rest for the remainder of the day and the following night. Marhabal, the cavalry leader, reckoned that they ought not to delay. 'No,' he said, 'so that you will appreciate what this battle has achieved, in five days time you will feast as a victor on the Capitol! Follow on! I shall go ahead with the cavalry, so that they will only hear of our approach after we have arrived.' This idea was too great and joyful for Hannibal to grasp immediately. And so he praised Marhabal's attitude; yet he needed time to consider his counsel. Then Maharbal said, 'Truly the gods do not give everything to the same man: you know how to win a victory, Hannibal, but you do not know how to use one.' This day's delay is widely believed to have saved the City and the empire.[7]

It is especially unfortunate that Polybius' surviving account breaks off after Cannae and we do not have his discussion of Hannibal's subsequent actions. Livy's view that Hannibal missed the opportunity of winning the war by not immediately moving on Rome has provoked varied comment. Some, including such notable soldiers as Field Marshal Montgomery, have agreed with the comment Livy attributed to Maharbal that Hannibal did not know how to a use a victory. Sometimes it is suggested that the Carthaginian army was ill prepared for siege warfare and the blame for this is laid at Hannibal's door, the claim being that it prevented him from finishing the campaign. Others, especially in recent years, have rejected Livy's view, claiming that a drive on Rome would have been difficult and unlikely to succeed, citing both practical and strategic arguments. Cannae is over 400km from Rome and only a small force of cavalry could even have dreamed of completing the journey in a mere five days. Advocates of this view argue that Rome was not undefended at this time, since sufficient troops could have reached the city before Hannibal. There may have been two 'urban' legions already in the process of being raised at Rome, whilst a detachment of 1,500 men was at Ostia and a legion destined to serve as marines with the fleet at Teanum. Another suggestion is that Hannibal simply could not have supplied his army if it had moved against Rome and then been forced to mount an assault or siege. The Carthaginians' lack of enthusiasm for sieges was not the result of lack of knowledge, but a result of Hannibal's desire never to be tied down in one place for the months necessary to reduce a strong city. Finally, that Hannibal did not move on Rome in 217 after Trasimene or 216 after Cannae, and only did so in 212 in an effort to draw the Romans away from his allies at Capua, is taken as proof that his plan never included the capture of the city itself. Instead Rome was to be persuaded to surrender by battlefield defeats and the break-up of its network of allies. In the weeks after Cannae this strategy would begin to bear fruit as much of Southern Italy defected to the Carthaginians.[8]

Although these claims are apparently plausible, many questionable assumptions underlie them. There is for instance a tendency to inflate the number and quality of troops available to defend Rome. We do not really know, for instance, whether the two urban legions had already been raised and organized by August. Similarly, whilst keeping his men and animals properly supplied is one of the first requirements of a commander, risks could well be taken in the short term if the military situation warranted it. Had Hannibal actually wanted to march on Rome, then it is unlikely that worries over supply would have prevented him. The central question is not whether or not he could then have captured the city by siege or direct attack, but whether the Romans would have resisted him at all. It was extremely difficult to capture a large and fortified city by assault in this period and neither the Romans nor the Carthaginians enjoyed much success whenever they made the attempt. Sieges were more likely to succeed, but took months or even years, the eight month siege of Saguntum being not untypical. Had the Romans resisted with even a garrison significantly smaller than some scholars believe was available, then Hannibal would be unlikely to have taken Rome and this failure would have robbed him of much of the prestige gained at Cannae. Yet this assumes that the Romans, confronted by the enemy outside their walls and with recent

catastrophe in their mind, would have fought and not simply capitulated in despair. That they acted so nonchalantly at the approach of the Punic army in 212, even auctioning off the plot of land on which Hannibal had pitched his camp and selling it for the full value, does not mean that they would have behaved in the same way in 216. The situation four years later was much more favourable for the Romans, who by that time had several strong, experienced armies in the field.[9]

Perhaps before closing this discussion of what Hannibal should, or should not, have done in the aftermath of Cannae, it is worth considering what he actually did. For some time he remained near the site of the battle, burying his many dead and caring for the wounded, and according to most versions also granting honourable burial to Paullus. Ten representatives were chosen from amongst the 8,000 Roman citizens held prisoner. These were to go to Rome and confirm the arrangements for their ransom already offered by Hannibal. Such negotiations to regulate the frequent ransom or exchange of prisoners appear to have been common throughout the First and Second Punic Wars, although they usually receive indirect mention in our sources. In this case, Hannibal sent with the ten captives one of his own staff, a certain Carthalo, probably the same man described elsewhere as the cavalry commander. He was sent with the express role of beginning negotiations if the Romans seemed at all inclined to seek peace.[10]

A view of part of the Sacra Via, the important ceremonial path into the centre of Rome as it passes through the Forum. Very few of the visible remains date to the third century BC. Yet this was already the heart of the City.

It was not at all unusual to begin the negotiations that would end a war under cover of talks dealing with the return of prisoners or retrieval of bodies. The majority of wars, especially between civilized states, were ended by negotiation, one side conceding defeat and accepting terms which acknowledged this, probably involving their giving up land or allies, paying a subsidy to the victor, and returning captives free whilst paying heavily for their own. Hannibal clearly entertained strong hopes that the Romans would now be ready to negotiate. In three years he had smashed successive armies sent against him, marching wherever he wished in Italy. Roman and allied casualties already totalled at least 100,000 men, well over a tenth of the Republic's military manpower. If the Romans could excuse their earlier defeats as a product of poor preparation, Cannae had been a trial of strength which they had carefully made ready for and actively sought. What more demonstration of Hannibal and Carthage's overwhelming superiority did the Romans require?[11]

The Romans had a short breathing space before the prisoners' representatives and Hannibal arrived. A dispatch arrived from Varro, informing the Senate that he was in the process of re-forming a force of about 10,000 men at Canusium. The report dispelled initial rumours that the entire army had been wiped out, but also gave details of the actual losses suffered at Cannae, which were only a little less appalling. Most families were in mourning, but the earlier restrictions on public displays of grief were enforced. The mood in the city remained on the verge of hysteria and, as after earlier disasters, fears developed that the proper rites to honour and propitiate the gods had been neglected. Two Vestal Virgins were accused of breaking their vows of chastity and condemned to the traditional punishment of being buried alive, although one committed suicide to avoid this fate. One of the girls' alleged lovers was flogged so badly that he died as a result. A delegation led by Fabius Pictor, later to become Rome's first prose historian, was sent to the great shrine of Apollo at Delphi to consult the oracle and gain guidance for how Rome could propitiate the gods and bring an end to the disasters besetting the city. In the meantime, a consultation of the Sybilline Books led to one of the few instances of human sacrifice ever practised at Rome; a Greek man and woman and a Gallic man and woman, presumably slaves, were buried alive under the Forum Boarium – the oldest of Rome's markets, which suggests that the rite was very ancient.

There was more bad news from Sicily where Rome's ally Syracuse was under threat from a Punic fleet. Yet the Senate began to plan for the future. Varro was instructed to return to the city once the experienced praetor Marcus

Claudius Marcellus arrived to take over his army. Marcus Junius Pera was appointed dictator, with Tiberius Sempronius Gracchus (soon to be twice consul and prove himself a gifted commander) as his *Magister Equitum*. This pair immediately began to levy new legions, taking men as young as 17 and also purchasing 8,000 slaves who were freed and enlisted. In time an army of four legions was created, armed in part from trophies, mostly Gallic weapons and armour, taken from the temples where they had been placed by triumphing generals in recent decades. Only 1,000 Roman cavalry could be raised, testifying to the heavy losses suffered by the equestrian order in the last two years. Rome was beginning to rebuild her strength, but this process would take a very long time. The mood became increasingly defiant, and when Varro returned to the city he was given something close to a hero's welcome, the Senate publicly thanking him 'for not having despaired of the Republic'.[12]

The Roman Senate held its nerve, perhaps encouraged by the activity it had set in motion. When news arrived of the approaching delegation of prisoners' representatives and Carthalo, the senate's response was immediate and unequivocal. Carthalo enjoyed the sanctity of an ambassador so was not harmed, but a *lictor* (one of the attendants of a Roman magistrate) was sent from the dictator to inform him that he would not be received and must depart from Roman territory before nightfall. There would be no negotiation with the enemy. The Romans had responded in exactly the same way earlier in the century when King Pyrrhus of Epirus had smashed their army in battle and sent an embassy to begin the discussion of a negotiated peace. The Romans were willing to negotiate only as victors, and demanded the admission of absolute defeat from their enemies even when this did not reflect the actual military situation. The Senate's response to the prisoners' requests matched this unyielding attitude. Not only did the State refuse to ransom them, but it also banned the men's families from raising the money privately. Livy noted that there were conflicting accounts of the fate of the ten delegates, but the most popular version was that they obeyed their oath to return to the enemy's camp and death or slavery, the Senate forcibly sending back those individuals who tried to escape from this obligation on a technicality.[13]

Hannibal chose not to march on Rome after Cannae. Both he and his army were utterly exhausted, for the battle had been long and hard fought under the heat of the summer sun. Hannibal himself had been very active throughout the battle, adding physical weariness to the mental stress of the days of manoeuvring and decision-making building up to the fighting. This probably contributed to his apparent lethargy, but the most probable reason for not moving instantly was his belief that this was unnecessary. Any other state in the classical world would surely have sought peace after a defeat on the scale of Cannae – probably just on its own and certainly in the wake of other serious defeats. War, as Hannibal had been raised to conceive of it and practise it, did not require the annihilation of the enemy, which was anyway seldom possible. Instead it required a demonstration that it was no longer in his interest to continue fighting. Once persuaded of this, a state or people conceded defeat and sought peace. This cultural assumption, more than anything else, probably explains why Hannibal did not move to threaten the city. In 216 BC the Romans did not obey Hellenistic conventions of war and accept defeat. Part of the reason why they continued to resist was the vast extent of the Republic's resources which allowed them to absorb the appalling casualties they had suffered. No other state had reserves of manpower on the same scale as Rome.

Even more important was the Romans' relentless attitude to war, which required every conflict to end in the absolute defeat either of the enemy or of themselves. It is possible that if Hannibal had moved directly on Rome after Cannae, the moral pressure exerted by the appearance of his army outside the city would have broken the Romans' spirit and ended the war. This may have been so, and with hindsight this was probably his best chance of victory. Yet such a move was also very dangerous and it is also possible that the Romans would have proved as stubborn as they did on other occasions, although none ever compared to such a threat. As with all the 'what if's' of history, we can never know.

THE LONG STRUGGLE, 216–201 BC

Though Hannibal can only have been disappointed by the Romans' refusal to admit defeat, there was much to encourage him in the months after Cannae. Soon most of Southern Italy defected to him, including the great city of Capua, whose population enjoyed Roman citizenship although without voting rights. The Carthaginian army ranged around the area, attacking the towns which resisted and encouraging local factions to join them. The losses of these allies were further blows to Roman prestige, an open acknowledgement of her weakness and inability to protect her friends. They also represented further reductions in her available manpower. In the North, the Gallic tribes of the Po valley remained in a state of rebellion and near the end of the year would wipe out an army of two legions led by the praetor and consul-elect Lucius Postumius Albinus. The praetor was killed and, according to Livy, beheaded, his gilded skull being subsequently used by the tribe's druids in their rituals.[14]

Mago Barca returned to Carthage to announce his brother's successes. On the floor of the Carthaginians' Ruling Council his attendants poured out the rings taken from dead or captured Roman equestrians, till thousands were piled up in heaps. He reinforced this visible proof of the enemy's massive losses with detailed accounts and asked that Hannibal be supported with more men and supplies. Livy, who throughout his account maintains that there was a significant party at Carthage opposed to Hannibal and the Barcids, has one Hanno mock these grandiloquent claims, wondering how much aid their commander would have requested if things were not going well. In the event, Hannibal was only ever to receive one significant reinforcement from Africa, although in part this lack may have been caused by his failure to secure a major port.[15]

The war in Italy changed after Cannae, for from then on Hannibal had bases to act from, but also allies to protect. There was little or no unity amongst his new-found allies, who had little in common with each other apart from their former link with Rome. Few were willing to commit significant numbers of men to fight outside their own lands, and all were firm in their belief that Hannibal was obliged to protect them from Roman depredations. The Romans sometimes had as many, or even more, troops in the field in Italy after Cannae, but never again were so many concentrated in a single field army. Instead between four and six independent armies were usually operating, occasionally moving together to support each other. They tried to avoid pitched battle with Hannibal's main army, save in the most favourable of circumstances, but everywhere raided and attacked his allies. As the years went by, the area loyal to Hannibal steadily declined as the Romans captured one town after another. This was a long process, and more than once Hannibal was able to surprise Roman forces and soundly beat them, most notably in the two battles at Herdonea in 212 and 210. The Romans suffered other major blows, such as when the city of Tarentum was betrayed to the enemy in 212; when both of the year's consuls were ambushed and killed (one actually dying of his wounds) in 208; and when some of her Latin allies declared themselves incapable of providing further soldiers and resources for the war effort in 209. Yet for all the pressure Hannibal put upon it, the Roman confederation did not collapse and continued to exert more and more of its massive power to regain losses.

The defections to Hannibal in the aftermath of Cannae.
The most serious loss was Capua, whose population enjoyed most of the rights of Roman citizens, although they were not able to vote or stand for election in Rome. The new allies gave Hannibal food and other aid and provided him with some troops, but also became a burden as they demanded that he defend them from the vengeful Romans. A more serious problem was his inability to secure a sizeable port.

Both Hannibal as a commander and his army as soldiers completely outclassed their Roman opponents in the early years of the war. This was not true of the other Punic leaders and their armies, who proved incapable of winning major battlefield victories over the Romans. During the war Roman military effectiveness steadily increased as soldiers and officers gained experience. This was to produce a generation when Roman commanders and their legions were of exceptionally high quality. When Hasdrubal and Mago Barca both led armies to join their brother in Italy, the former was swiftly overwhelmed and his army destroyed, the latter stopped and defeated in Northern Italy. However, at first the quality of the new Roman

PENNINES

**Italian defections to
Hannibal in the aftermath of Cannae**

Defections to Hannibal

Hannibals route out of Italy

Gerunium

Luceria

Arpi

Allifae

Salapia

Adriatic Sea

Aecae

Herdonia

Canusium

S a m n i u m

A p u l i a

Capua ⊙ *Recaptured
in 211*

Beneventum

Venusia

Neapolis

Nuceria

Compsa

*Captured in 212,
recaptured in 209*

Brundisium

⊙ Tarentum

L u c a n i a

Metapontum

Grumentum

Heraclea

Velia

Thurii

*T y r r h e n i a n
S e a*

Consentia

Petelia

*Hannibal withdraws
from Italy in 203*

Croton

N

0   50   100 Miles

0   50   100   Km

B r u t t i u m

Caulonia

Locri

Messina

*M e d i t e r r a n e a n
S e a*

Rhegium

armies was demonstrated against opponents other than Hannibal. Even during the worst crisis in Italy the Senate continued to send resources to prosecute the war on other fronts, in Spain and Sicily and also, when Hannibal entered an alliance with King Philip V of Macedon, in Greece. In Macedonia the war, known today as the First Macedonian War, would end in stalemate and an unsatisfactory peace treaty (so much so that one of the first Roman acts after ending the war with Carthage was to enter a new bout of conflict with Philip). In Sicily and Spain the Romans would eventually win outright victories, expelling the Carthaginians from the regions.

Finally, in 204, a Roman consul who had made his name in Spain led an invasion army from Sicily into Africa. This was Publius Cornelius Scipio, the same young man who had saved his father's life at Ticinus and assumed command of the survivors after Cannae. At the heart of his army were two legions formed from the fugitives of Cannae, and later reinforced by men from the disasters at Herdonea. From the beginning the Senate had decided to treat these men harshly, sending them to Sicily and refusing to allow them to return to Italy. It was one of the great ironies of the war that it was these legions under Scipio which faced Hannibal after the Carthaginians had recalled his army from Italy to protect their city. At Zama in 202 BC it was a well trained and highly experienced Roman army which faced a larger, but very mixed Carthaginian force, whose members had had little opportunity to train together. Also, unlike all Hannibal's earlier victories in Italy, the Carthaginians were outnumbered in cavalry. The resulting battle was a tough slogging match, but in the end Hannibal's infantry were attacked from the front by the Roman infantry and from the rear by Roman and allied cavalry, much of it drawn from the Numidian tribes. On this occasion Scipio employed no tactics as imaginative as Hannibal's at Cannae, but the result was

The battle of Zama. Importantly Hannibal was outnumbered in cavalry. When the massed elephant charge failed to disorder the Roman line, both wings of Punic cavalry were swept away. The Romans advanced and ground through the first and second lines of Carthaginian infantry. The battle was decided in the end by the return of the Roman cavalry who took the Punic third line in the rear. Though Hannibal did not suffer as heavy losses as he had inflicted on the Romans at Cannae, the Carthaginians lacked Rome's stubborn will to continue in any circumstances and surrendered.

N

Laelius

Scipio

Lanes left through the
Roman formation to
allow elephants to
charge straight through

*Hannibal's third line
kept several hundred
metres back as reserve*

Hannibal

Punic camp

n camp

Masinissa

The Battle of Zama, 202 BC

Carthaginians

Carthaginian
cavalry

Gallic & Ligurian
infantry

Hanibal's
Veterans

Libyan & Punic
infantry

Elephants

Romans

Roman cavalry

Numidian cavalry

Roman infantry

This pillar,
erected in
the nineteenth
century by
the Italian
government to
commemorate
the battle of
Cannae, stands
near the ruins of
the town on the
hill overlooking
the battlefield.
The ruins of the
town date to the
Imperial period.

the same, for the Punic army was utterly defeated. Carthage had few resources left. More importantly there was little will to continue the struggle. Unlike the Romans in 216, they soon opened negotiations for peace, accepting the terms imposed by the Romans upon them. The Second Punic War was over.

Hannibal survived the defeat of Zama. In the years after the war he won the high office of suffete at Carthage and did much to encourage the revival of his city's prosperity. Yet a combination of political rivals at Carthage and a growing desire for revenge amongst many Roman senators eventually forced him into exile. He became a mercenary commander, fleeing to the courts of a succession of monarchs in the Hellenistic East, especially those hostile to Rome. Eventually, hunted by Roman agents, he took his own life in Bithynia in 183.[16]

CANNAE IN HISTORY

Cannae was Hannibal's greatest triumph, but there was nothing inevitable about the course of the battle in spite of the brilliance of his plan. There was no guarantee that Hasdrubal's cavalry would be able to smash through the Roman horse quickly enough, for the confined space between the River Aufidius and the infantry in the centre limited the advantage derived from their numerical superiority. Hasdrubal was required not simply to rout the Roman cavalry, but also then to rally his men, keeping them in good enough order to perform further complex manoeuvres and mount other attacks. Throughout history it has been the exception rather than the rule for cavalry to operate in such a controlled manner, for the very speed and exhilaration of the charge foster disorder. Similarly, Hannibal knew that defeat of the Gallic and Spanish infantry in the centre was inevitable, but required them to hold out for just the right amount of time. If they broke too soon, before the Romans had become wearied and disordered in a prolonged combat, then the enemy foot would break through with such force that it was unlikely the Libyans would have the power to stop them. In the event the very numbers of the Roman infantry, and the deep and closely packed formation they had adopted, worked against them, merging the individual maniples into an unwieldy crowd utterly incapable of reacting to a changing situation. This process took time, and until its later stages the Roman foot continued to create a massive forward momentum, which there was no assurance that either the first Punic line or the Libyan reserves would be able to halt. In the event everything went Hannibal's way, but things might easily have been different.

The Punic Wars, and Hannibal in particular, captured the imagination of many generations. This sixteenth century work, now in the Pushkin Museum in Moscow, gives a fanciful interpretation of the battle of Zama.

Cannae has long held a peculiar fascination with soldiers and scholars alike. As recently as the Gulf War in 1991, the UN Commander General Schwartzkopf claimed to have drawn inspiration for his brief and devastatingly effective land offensive from Hannibal. During the Second World War Rommel was not the only German officer to desire or claim to have inflicted a 'Cannae' on the enemy. Earlier in the century Von Schlieffen, the architect of the plan used for the German invasion of France in 1914, was obsessed with Hannibal's victory, studying the battle time and time again for inspiration as he painstakingly drafted and re-drafted his grand design. The resultant plan bore only a superficial similarity to the Carthaginian's tactics at Cannae and was conceived on an infinitely grander scale. It also failed.

Other battles where an enemy has been enveloped on both sides, surrounded and suffered terrible casualties are sometimes likened to Cannae, whether their outcome was the product of chance or deliberate design. The battle of the Falaise Gap in August 1944 is one such victory, but, when it is remembered that this was the culmination of months of fighting in Normandy and fought between armies of many hundreds of thousands over a huge frontage, the similarities with the single day's fighting on a narrow plain beside the Aufidius seem to recede. Cannae was a battle very much of its time. It was a formal affair, preceded by days of cautious manoeuvring, as the rival commanders strove to give their own soldiers confidence and as many advantages as they could. Battles were too important to be risked lightly, though both sides expected them to be the decisive element in a campaign. Hannibal excelled in this type of fighting and even here, where the actual battlefield was chosen by his Roman opponent, he was able to turn this to his advantage. He won because he was able to exploit the superiority of his own army and senior subordinates and overcome the numerical advantage of his opponents. His tactics were an ingenious and imaginative response to the local situation, but it was only through his own and his officers' leadership and skill, along with the bravery of his soldiers, that they proved successful.

NOTES

CHAPTER 1

1 For an overview of the Mediterranean world in this period see A. Toynbee, *Hannibal's Legacy. Vol. 1* (Oxford, 1965), pp. 20–83; for Carthage, its history and culture see G. Picard and C. Picard, *Carthage* (rev. ed.: London, 1987), and S. Lancel, *Carthage* (Oxford, 1995); for Rome's origins, society and history see T. Cornell, *The Beginnings of Rome* (London, 1995), and M. Crawford, *The Roman Republic* (Glasgow, 1978).

2 On the First Punic War see J. Lazenby, *The First Punic War* (London, 1995), B. Caven, *The Punic Wars* (1980), pp. 1–84, and A. Goldsworthy, *The Punic Wars* (London, 2000), pp. 65–140.

3 On the causes of the Second Punic War see J. Lazenby, *Hannibal's War* (Warminster, 1978), pp.

1–28, Goldsworthy (2000), pp. 143–166, and especially J. Rich, 'The origins of the Second Punic War', in T. Cornell, B. Rankov, and P. Sabin, *The Second Punic War: A Reappraisal* (London, 1996), pp. 1–37.

4 Sosylus Hannibal's tutor in Greek, Cornelius Nepos, *Hannibal* 13. 3.

5 Hannibal's oath, Polybius 3. 11. 5–12. 4.

6 The size of Hannibal's army, Polybius 3. 35. 1, Appian, *Hannibalic War* 1. 4. For a detailed discussion of the army's size at various stages of the campaign see Appendix 1. For a fuller discussion of Punic strategy see Goldsworthy (2000), pp. 130–133, 152–153.

7 Hannibal's character, Polybius 9. 22. 1–26. 11, Livy 22. 4. 2–5. 2.

8 For more detailed accounts and discussions of the campaigns in 218–217 BC, see Lazenby (1978), pp. 29–73, Caven (1980), pp. 98–132, and Goldsworthy (2000), pp. 167–196.

9 For a perceptive discussion of the 'Fabian strategy' see P. Erdkamp, 'Polybius, Livy and the Fabian Strategy', *Ancient Society* 23 (1992), pp. 127–147.

CHAPTER 2

1 For good introductions to the development of the Roman army see L. Keppie, *The Making of the Roman Army* (London, 1984), E. Gabba, *Republican Rome: The Army and Allies* (Berkeley, 1976), A. Goldsworthy, *Roman Warfare* (London, 2000), and F. Adcock, *The Roman Art of War under the Republic* (Cambridge, 1960).

2 Polybius' description of the army, 6. 19. 1–42. 6; for a discussion see Walbank, *Polybius* 1 (Oxford, 1970), pp. 697–723. The basic study of the evidence for the early Roman army is E. Rawson, 'The literary sources for the pre-Marian Roman Army', *Papers of the British School at Rome* 39 (1971), pp. 13–31. For the 'reform' of 211, see the unconvincing arguments in M. Samuels, 'The Reality of Cannae', *Militärgeschichtliche Mitteilungen* 47 (1990), pp. 7–31.

3 Polybius 6. 25. 1–11; on the saddle see P. Connolly, 'The Roman saddle', in M. Dawson (ed.), *Roman Military Equipment: The Accoutrements of War. BAR* 336 (Oxford, 1987), pp. 7–27, and A. Hyland, *Training the Roman Cavalry* (Gloucester, 1993), pp. 45–51.

4 Polybius 6. 24. 1–9.

5 Polybius 6. 23. 1–16; for weapons and armour see M. Feugere, *Les Armes des romains de la république à l'antiquité tardive* (Paris, 1993), M. Bishop and J. Coulston, *Roman Military Equipment* (London, 1993), and P. Connolly, *Greece and Rome at War* (London, 1981) and 'Pilum, gladius and pugio in the Late Republic', *Journal of Roman Military Equipment Studies* 8 (1997), pp. 41–57. On the find of a probable Roman *scutum* see W. Kimmig, 'Ein Keltenschild aus Aegypten', *Germania* 24 (1940), pp. 106–111.

6 On velites Polybius 6. 22. 1–4. On legionary numbers see A. Goldsworthy, *The Punic Wars* (London, 2000), pp. 50–51.

7 See M. Bell, 'Tactical Reform in the Roman Republican Army', *Historia* 14 (1965), pp. 404–422, Goldsworthy, *Punic Wars* (2000), pp. 53–4, 57–62, and *The Roman Army at War 100 BC–AD 200* (Oxford, 1996), pp. 138–140, 179–180.

8 See Goldsworthy, *The Punic Wars* (2000), pp. 36–44, 52–3, for an introduction to Roman politics and a discussion of commanders.

9 Various strengths of allied cohorts: 460, Livy 23. 17. 11; 500, Livy 23. 17. 8; 570, Livy 23. 19; 600, Livy 28. 45. We do not know if these were 'paper' or actual strengths.

10 Disputes between joint commanders, see Polybius 3. 70. 1–12, 94. 7–10, 100. 1–105. 11.

11 Roman manpower see Polybius 2. 24. 1–17, with discussion in Walbank 1 (1970), pp. 196–203 and P. Brunt, *Italian Manpower* (Oxford, 1971).

12 For the Carthaginian military system in general see Goldsworthy, *The Punic Wars* (2000), pp.

30–36; for a discussion of the poor evidence for Punic armies see J. Lazenby, *Hannibal's War* (Warminster, 1978), pp. 14–16; for an interesting discussion of Gallic, Spanish and other tribal contingents in Hannibal's army see L. Rawlings, 'Celts, Spaniards, and Samnites: Warriors in a Soldiers' War', in T. Cornell, B. Rankov, and P. Sabin, *The Second Punic War: A Reappraisal* (London, 1996), pp. 81–95. D. Head, *Armies of the Macedonian and Punic Wars* attempts to reconstruct Punic equipment and organisation in some detail and presents a thorough survey of the scant evidence, but inevitably many of his conclusions are highly conjectural.

13 The armies left to defend Spain and Africa, Polybius 3. 33. 5–16.

14 *Lonchophoroi*, e.g. Polybius 3. 72. 3, 83. 3, 84. 14; equipping Libyans with Roman arms, 3. 87. 3.

15 Marriage alliances between Punic aristocrats and Numidian royalty, e.g. Polybius 1. 78. 1–9, Livy 29. 23. 2-8; in Spain, *DS* 25. 12, Livy 24. 51. 7, Silius Italicus 3. 97, 106.

16 500 Numidians, Livy 26. 38. 11–14; Libyans at Saguntum, Livy 21. 11. 8; Gauls at Tarentum, Polybius 8. 30. 1; *speiras* at Cannae, Polybius 3. 114. 4, cf. 6. 24. 5.

17 Emphasis on the greater experience of Hannibal's men compared to the Romans in 218, Polybius 3. 70. 9–11; Spanish units interspersed with Gauls at Cannae, 3. 114. 4; poor march discipline of Gauls, 3. 79. 6–8; Tarentum, 8. 30. 1–4, Livy 24. 9. 16.

CHAPTER 3

1 Polybius' description of Paullus, 3. 107. 8; the Illyrian War, Polybius 3. 19. 13, Livy 22. 35. 3, 40. 349. 11, Frontinus *Strategemata* 4. 1. 45.

2 The bill to grant Minucius equal power with Fabius, Livy 22. 25. 1–19; Varro's character and career, 22. 25. 18–26. 4.

3 Livy 22. 34. 2–35. 4; for a discussion suggesting a closer link between Varro and Paullus see J. Lazenby, *Hannibal's War* (Warminster, 1978), pp. 73–5.

4 For narratives emphasizing factions see B. Caven, *The Punic Wars* (London, 1980), pp. 20, 83–4, and to a lesser extent Lazenby (1978), pp. 4, 108. H. Scullard, *Roman politics 220–150 BC* (London, 1951) represents an extreme form of this view.

5 Polybius 3. 107. 9–15 with discussion in F. Walbank, *Polybius* 1 (Oxford, 1970), pp. 439–440, 440; Telamon 2. 24. 3, Walbank 1 (1970), p. 199.

6   Livy 22. 36. 1–5; B. Caven, *The Punic Wars* (London, 1980), pp. 134–141, and P. Brunt, *Italian Manpower* (Oxford, 1971), p. 419 are argue for the lower total; vague comments attributed to Paullus, Polybius 3. 109. 5, Hannibal, Livy 22. 40. 7, 41. 5, suggest the higher total, but should not be pushed too far.

7   For Fabius' legions and their origins see Walbank 1, pp. 410–411; Appian *Hannibalic War* 8 claims that Servilius Geminus had taken over Sempronius Longus' legions in 217.

8   Livy 22. 38. 2–5; for the *sacramentum* see B. Campbell, *The Emperor and the Roman Army* (Oxford, 1984), pp. 19–32.

9   The election of the praetors and their distinguished records, see Livy 22. 35. 5–7.

10 Lazenby (1978), p. 75, and Brunt (1971), p. 419.

11 Polybius 3. 108. 2–109. 13.

12 Livy 22. 38. 6–40. 4, 41. 13, 49. 6–12, cf. Plutarch *Fabius Maximus* 14–16, Appian, *Hann.* 17–19.

13 Livy 22. 40. 7–8.

14 See P. Erdkamp, 'Polybius, Livy and the Fabian Strategy', *Ancient Society* 23 (1992), pp. 127–147 for a discussion of the evidence.

15 Plutarch, *Lucullus* 11. 1; Fabius' cautious and stubborn nature see Plutarch, *Fabius Maximus passim,* esp. 1 and 25.

16 Hannibal waiting for the harvest to ripen, Polybius 3. 107. 1–2 with comments in Walbank 1 (1970), p. 441; the tradition that the consuls joined the army before Hannibal moved, see Livy 22. 41. 4–43. 8 with comments in Lazenby (1978), p. 76.

17 Polybius' belief that Hannibal's primary aim in 216 was to fight a battle, 3. 107. 2–3; the Carthaginian spy, Livy 22. 33. 1–2; on intelligence gathering in general see M. Austin and B. Rankov, *Exploratio* (London, 1995).

18 Livy 22. 40. 6.

19 Gisgo see Plutarch, *Fabius Maximus* 15. 2–3; the Romans' careful scouting, Livy 22. 44. 1.

20 Polybius 3. 110. 1–3.

21 Polybius 3. 110. 4–11; Lazenby (1978), p. 77 doubted that it would have been impossible for the Romans to withdraw, but does not provide a convincing argument to support this.

22 Polybius 3. 111. 1–11.

23 Polybius 3. 112. 1–5.

24 Polybius 3. 112. 6–113. 1.

CHAPTER 4

1 Polybius 3. 113. 1–6, Livy 22. 45. 5–46. 1.

2 Polybius 3. 112. 1–5, Livy 22. 44. 5–45. 4.

3 For the suggestion that Paullus was in fact in command see P. Connolly, *Greece and Rome at War* (1981), pp. 184–6.

4 Polybius' description of the battlefield, see Walbank, *Polybius* 1 (Oxford, 1970), pp. 435–8. When I visited the site in the summer of 1999, the actual line of the river conformed to none of the maps I had with me.

5 K. Lehmann, *Klio* 15 (1917), p. 162, and *Klio* (1931), pp. 70–99; and H. Delbrück (trans. W. Renfroe), *History of the Art of War 1* (Nebraska, 1975), pp. 324–5.

6 J. Kromayer & G. Veith, *Antike Schlachtfelder* (1903–31) III, 1, pp. 278–388, followed by *inter alia* J. Lazenby, *Hannibal's War* (Warminster, 1978), p. 77–8.

7 P. Connolly, *Greece and Rome at War* (London, 1981), p. 184.

8 Livy 22. 36. 4.

9 For the general accounts of each side's deployment see Polybius 3. 113. 2–114. 8, Livy 22. 45. 6–9; for a detailed discussion of strengths see Appendix 1.

10 Polybius 3. 117. 8–9; for their possible identity see Lazenby (1978), pp. 79–80, Connolly (1981), p. 187; examples of *triarii* guarding the camp include Livy 35. 4 and 44. 37, but in contrast to Cannae, in neither case did the army plan to fight a battle.

11 Issus, Polybius 12. 18. 2–4.

12 For a discussion of formations see A. Goldsworthy, *The Roman Army at War* (Oxford, 1996), pp. 176–183; Vegetius 3. 14–15 allocated a frontage of 1m (3 feet) and a depth of 2.1m (7 feet) to a Roman legionary. Elsewhere Polybius claimed that each legionary occupied 1.8m (6 feet) square, but the passage is heavily stylized and seems improbable; 18. 30. 5–11.

13 E.g. Lazenby (1978), pp. 79–80, Connolly (1981), pp. 184–7, and Delbrück (1975), pp. 325–7.

14 Greek practice of putting bravest in the front and rear ranks, see Xenophon, *Mem.* 3. 19, Aescepiodotus, *Tactics* 14. 6; on the role of the *optio* see M. Speidel, *The Framework of an Imperial Legion* (Cardiff, 1992), pp. 24–6.

15 Delbrück (1975), p. 325.

16 Trebia, Polybius 3. 74. 3–6; Trasimene, Polybius 84. 3–7; Roman emphasis on *bia* Polybius 1. 37. 7–10.

17 At Metaurus in 207 BC the consul C. Claudius Nero controlled the right, the praetor

L. Porcius Licinus the centre and the other consul M. Livius Drusus Salinator the left, in spite of the fact that the battle was fought under his command, Livy 27. 98.

18 Crossing the river in two columns, Polybius 3. 113. 6.

19 Polybius 3. 114. 4

20 Zama, Polybius 15. 9. 1–11. 12, Livy 30. 32. 1–33. 11.

21 Ecnomus as the model for Cannae see W. Tarn, *Hellenistic military and naval developments* (Cambridge, 1930), p. 165, J. Thiel, *A history of Roman sea-power before the Second Punic War* (Amsterdam, 1954), pp. 120–1, and Walbank 1 (1970), p. 87, as well as the refutation of this view in J. Lazenby, *The First Punic War* (London, 1996), pp. 94–5 and p. 185, n. 20.

22 Ennius *Fragment* 282.

23 Polybius 3. 115. 1, Livy 22. 47. 1. On missile ranges see Goldsworthy (1996), pp. 183–190.

24 For an example of a protracted skirmish resulting in few fatalities and no decisive result, Josephus *Bellum Judaicum* 3. 150–54; studies of twentieth century combat, see S.L.A. Marshall, *Men against Fire* (New York, 1947), esp. pp. 51–4, 65.

25 Telamon, Polybius 2. 30. 1–4; Galatia, 189 BC, Livy 38. 21; for the supposed reform of 211 and the poor quality of Roman skirmishers before this date, see M. Samuels, 'The Reality of Cannae', *Militärgeschichtliche Mitteilungen* 47 (1990), pp. 7–31.

26 Livy 22. 49. 1.

27 Polybius 3. 115. 2–4, Livy 22. 47. 1–3; for a discussion of cavalry combat see Goldsworthy (1996), pp. 235–244.

28 Plutarch, *Fabius Maximus* 16, Livy 22. 49. 2–5, Appian *Hann.* 24.

29 Ticinus, Polybius 3. 65. 5–11; infantry interspersed with cavalry, Caesar *Bellum Gallicum* 1. 48, 7. 36, 7. 80, *Bellum Civile* 2. 34, 3. 75, 3. 84, *African War* 20, 61, 78, and discussion in Goldsworthy (1996), pp. 242–4.

30 Livy 22. 47. 3.

31 Polybius 3. 116. 5, Livy 22. 48. 1–4, Appian, *Hann.* 20, 22–3.

32 Noise, Polybius 1. 34. 2, 15. 12. 8; importance of appearance, Caesar, *Bellum Gallicum* 2. 21, Plutarch, *Lucullus* 27. 5 and discussion in Goldsworthy (1996), pp. 192–7.

33 Polybius 3. 114. 2–4, 115. 5–7, Livy 22. 46. 5–6, 47. 4–5; Germans, Tacitus *Germania* 3.

34 Gaesatae, Polybius 2. 28. 8, 29. 7–9.

35 On the range of the *pilum*, see J. Vechère de Reffyre, 'Les Armes d'Alise', *RA* 2 (1864), p. 342, and M. Junkelmann, *Die Legionen des Augustus* (Mainz, 1991), p. 188;

Josephus *Bellum Judaicum* 3. 259, 266, 4. 20. For a detailed study of the use of missiles by Roman infantry see A. Zhmodikov, 'Roman Republican Heavy Infantrymen in Battle (IV–II centuries BC), *Historia* 49. 1 (2000), pp. 67–78, and also the comments in Goldsworthy (1996), pp. 192–201.

36   For discussions of infantry combat see Goldsworthy (1996), pp. 191–227, and see P. Sabin, 'The mechanics of battle in the Second Punic War', in Cornell, Rankov and Sabin (1996), pp. 59–79, esp. 64–73; for a detailed discussion of the most extensive set of grave finds see B. Thordeman, *Armour from the battle of Wisby 1361.* vols. 1–2 (Stockholm, 1939), esp. vol. 1, pp. 94–5, 160–194.

37   Hoplite warfare see V. Hanson, *The Western Way of War* (New York, 1989), J. Lazenby, 'The Killing Zone', in V. Hanson (ed.), *Hoplites* (New York, 1991), pp. 87–109, and A. Goldsworthy, 'The *Othismos*, Myths and Heresies', *War in History* 4 (1997), pp. 1–26.

38   Plutarch, *Cato the Elder* 1; multiple head wounds, see M. Wheeler, *Maiden Castle, Dorset* (1943), p. 352 as well as Thordeman (1939) *passim.*

39   Centurions, Polybius 6. 24. 9; senior officers at Cannae, Polybius 3. 116. 1–4, Livy 22. 49. 2. For a detailed discussion of the role of Roman commanders at a later period see Goldsworthy (1996), pp. 149–163.

40   Livy 22. 47. 5–6.

41   For a full discussion of casualties see Appendix 2.

42   Polybius 3. 115. 6.

43   Polybius 3. 115. 8–10, Livy 22. 47. 7–10.

44   Polybius 3. 116. 5–8, Livy 22. 48. 5–6.

45   E.g. B. Caven, *The Punic Wars* (London, 1980), p. 139, Lazenby (1978), p. 84, Connolly (1981), p. 188. For a vivid attempt to reconstruct this final phase see V. Hanson, 'Cannae', in R. Cowley (ed.) *Experience of War* (New York, 1992), pp. 42–9.

46   E.g. Connolly (1981), p. 187.

47   On the proper behaviour for soldiers and commanders in defeat see N. Rosenstein, *Imperatores Victi* (Berkeley, 1990).

48   Ranks packed too densely so that the men in front could retreat were always a source of especially high casualties, e.g. Caesar, *Bellum Gallicum* 5. 43, Tacitus, *Annals* 2. 20, 14. 37, Josephus, *Bellum Judaicum* 3. 271–5.

49   Death of Paullus, Polybius 3. 116. 9, Livy 22. 49. 6–12, cf. Plutarch, *Fabius Maximus* 16.

50   Polybius 3. 117. 1–6, Livy 22. 49. 13–50. 3, 52. 6; for a full discussion see Appendix 2.

CHAPTER 5

1　Livy 22. 51. 5–9; for British casualties on the Somme see M. Middlebrook, *The First Day of the Somme* (London, 1971), pp. 262–4 and also see Appendix 2.

2　Livy 22. 50. 4–12, 52. 4, and for the lower estimate see Frontinus, *Strategemata* 4. 5. 7.

3　Polybius 3. 117. 7–12, Livy 22. 52. 1–6.

4　Polybius 3. 117. 2, Livy 22. 50. 3, 52. 7–53. 13.

5　Livy 22. 54. 1–6.

6　Livy 22. 54. 7–56. 8, Plutarch, *Fabius Maximus* 17–18.

7　Livy 22. 51. 1–4.

8　For useful surveys of the evidence and arguments claiming that it was never Hannibal's intention to attack Rome see J. Lazenby, *Hannibal's War* (Warminster, 1978), pp. 85–6, and "Was Hannibal Right?", in T. Cornell, B. Rankov, and P. Sabin (edd.) *The Second Punic War: A Reappraisal*, BICS Supplement 67 (London, 1996), 39–48, and also H. Delbrück (trans. J. Renfroe), *History of the Art of War 1* (Nebraska, 1975), pp. 336–44; for arguments based on logistics see J. Shean, 'Hannibal's mules: the logistical limitations of Hannibal's army and the battle of Cannae, 216 BC', *Historia* 45 (1996), pp. 159–87.

9　Livy 26. 11. 6.

10　Livy 22. 58. 1–61. 15.

11　See A. Goldsworthy, *The Punic Wars* (London, 2000), pp. 216–19, and B.D. Hoyos "Hannibal: What kind of genius?", *Greece and Rome* 30 (1983), pp. 171–80, esp. 177–8; use of negotiations over casualties to initiate peace talks see Livy 33. 11–12.

12　N. Rosenstein, *Imperatores Victi* (Berkeley, 1990), pp. 139–40, Livy 22. 57. 10–12, 61. 14–5, 23. 14. 1–4.

13　Livy 22. 53. 7–9; refusal to negotiate with Pyrrhus, Plutarch, *Pyrrhus* 18–20.

14　For general accounts of the war after Cannae see Lazenby (1978), p. 87+, B. Caven, *The Punic Wars* (London, 1980), p. 140, and Goldsworthy (2000), p. 219; for Postumius' defeat see Polybius 3. 118. 6, Livy 23. 24. 6–13.

15　Livy 23. 12. 1–2.

16　Livy 39. 51

APPENDIX 1: Numbers

A: HANNIBAL'S ARMY

1. The March to Italy

Date	Detachments and Losses:	Source
Spring 218 setting out from New Carthage	12,000 cavalry & 90,000 infantry + 37 elephants	Polybius 3. 35. 1 & Livy 21. 23. 1 Appian *Hann.* 4
Summer 218 left in Eastern Spain	1000 cavalry and 10,000 infantry at least 11,000 other less reliable troops sent home	Polybius 3. 35. 5–6 Livy 21. 23. 3–6
Summer 218 after crossing the Pyrenees	9,000 cavalry and 50,000 infantry	Polybius 3. 35. 7–8
Summer 218 after crossing the River Rhône	8,000 cavalry and 38,000 infantry	Polybius 3. 60. 5
Late autumn 218 in Northern Italy after crossing the Alps	6,000 cavalry (mixed Numidian and Spanish) and 20,000 infantry (12,000 Libyan and 8,000 Spanish)	Polybius 3. 56. 4

Of these figures Polybius specifically attributes the last set to an inscription erected by Hannibal on the Lacinian Peninsula (3. 56. 4). He does not appear to have derived the other numbers from such a reliable source, and this has sometimes led to these being questioned by historians.[1] Ultimately it is impossible to know whether the numbers given for the early stages of the expedition are accurate or not. If they are correct, then Hannibal detached around 22,000 men before leaving Spain and lost around 4,000 cavalry and 50,000 infantry through combat, desertion, disease and attrition in the five months it took him to march from New Carthage to Italy. The losses may be broken down for each stage of the journey as follows:

1. New Carthage to the Pyrenees   21,000 men
2. Pyrenees to the Rhône   13,000 men
3. Rhône to Italy   20,000 men

Polybius comments that Hannibal had lost nearly half of his army in the last phase of the march, mostly in crossing the Alps (3. 60. 5). Losses amongst baggage animals had been proportionally even higher (3.56. 2). However, it is noticeable that throughout the march his cavalry had suffered a lower percentage loss than his infantry, 50% compared to 88%. This is surprising, since horses will usually break down before men. The cavalry were very much the élite of Hannibal's army and it is probable that he took particular care of them. This, perhaps along with higher morale, may explain this marked difference.

Whether or not these figures are correct, all of our sources believed that Hannibal's army suffered very heavily on the march to Italy, especially during the passage of the Alps. Probably the bulk of such losses were as a result of physical weakness or disease which made it impossible for men to keep pace with the column, or through desertion. If Hannibal's army was initially as large as Polybius believed, then the overwhelming bulk of its manpower most probably consisted of recently recruited Spaniards. Tribal warfare did not require the same stamina as such a long march and probably did little to prepare warriors for its rigours.

Polybius provides us with the most plausible estimate of Hannibal's strength and losses. However, Livy says that there was a very wide range of numbers given by his sources. Lucius Cincius Alimentus was one of Rome's first historians, a senator who fought in these campaigns and was at one stage taken prisoner by the Carthaginians. He claimed that he had heard Hannibal say that he had lost 36,000 men and an enormous number of horses and baggage animals after crossing the Rhône. Alimentus estimated that Hannibal had 10,000 cavalry and 80,000 infantry on arrival in Italy. However, as Livy points out, this figure is of little value for it included the many Gallic and Ligurian tribesmen who would rally to Hannibal's cause after his crossing of the Alps (21. 38. 2–5).

2. The Campaigns in Italy, November 218–spring 216 BC
(a) The battle of Trebia, December 218 BC:
  (i) *Overall total* - 10,000 cavalry (6,000 Spanish and Numidian + 4,000 Gauls) 28,000

infantry (8,000 skirmishers and 20,000 close order infantry of whom at least 12,000 were African, 8,000 Spanish and 8,000 Gauls).

Sources - Polybius 3. 72. 7–9, Livy 21. 55. 2–4.

(ii) *Losses* – unspecified, but relatively light amongst the Africans and Spanish, and heavier amongst the Gauls. However in the winter months many men and horses died along with all of the army's elephants (Polybius 3. 74. 10–11).

(b) The battle of Lake Trasimene, June 217 BC:

(i) *Overall total* - unspecified, but it is clear that Hannibal had been joined by a significant number of Gallic tribesmen before he left Cisalpine Gaul. He must have had at least the 50,000 men present at Cannae since he received no reinforcements before that battle.

(ii) *Losses* – 1,500, mostly Gauls and 30 senior officers (Polybius 3. 85. 5). 2,500 in the battle and 'many' subsequently of their wounds (Livy 22. 7. 3).

(c) Gerunium, autumn 217 BC

(i) *Overall total* - not stated

(ii) Casualties - some of Livy's sources claimed that 6,000 Carthaginians were killed (22. 24. 14). Polybius says vaguely that many were killed, but also claims that the greater part of Hannibal's army was not present (3. 102. 8). It is probable that the figure of 6,000 is hugely exaggerated.

(d) The battle of Cannae, August 216 BC:

(i) *Overall total* - 10,000 cavalry (maximum of 6,000 Numidians and Spanish, and the remainder Gauls) 40,000 infantry (perhaps 8,000 skirmishers and 32,000 close order foot: absolute maximum of 12,000 Africans and 8,000 Spanish (and probably fewer) and the remainder Gauls

Sources - Polybius 3. 114. 5, Livy 22. 46. 6.

B: The Roman Army at Cannae

1. Numbers:

(i) Polybius' version (3. 107. 9–15, 113. 5):

Eight legions each of 5,000 infantry and 300 cavalry, supported by the same number of allied foot and more cavalry.

Total = 80,000 infantry and 6,000 cavalry (2,400 Roman, if all legions were at full strength, and the remainder supplied by Latin and Italian allies).

(ii) Livy's alternatives (22. 36. 1–5):

(a) 10,000 new soldiers enlisted as replacements - total *c.* 50,000–55,000.

(b) Four new legions formed to add to the four already at Gerunium (each legion either 4,000 foot and 200 horse or 4,200 foot and 200 horse)- total *c.* 64,000–67,200 infantry and 4,800 cavalry.

(c) A variation on (b) - four exceptionally strong legions enrolled, consisting of 5,000 foot and 300 horse, and supplements sent to bring the existing legions up to the same strength. Twice as many cavalry and an equal number of infantry also supplied by the allies - total *c.* 80,000 infantry and 7,200 cavalry.

Livy's narrative clearly assumes that estimate (c) was correct, but some scholars have preferred the lower estimate. Brunt stated that the lower estimate is to be preferred '... because the success of Hannibal's tactics at Cannae is unintelligible if the Roman forces outnumbered his own by two to one'. As we have seen in the main text, the opposite is true, for the deep formation adopted by the Roman centre makes no sense if the Romans had roughly the same number of infantry as the enemy.[2]

2. Identity of the legions in 216 BC

Assuming that Polybius was correct and there were eight legions at Cannae, half had been raised in late 217 or early 216 and the other four were the troops formerly commanded by the dictator. These consisted of:

1. The two legions formed by Fabius Maximus (Livy 22. 11. 2–3) in 217.

2. The two legions formerly commanded by Servilius Geminus. The cavalry of this army had been wiped out in Centenius' disaster in the days after Trasimene. Geminus had taken command in March 217 of half the army which had re-formed after Trebia. Flaminius took over the two legions commanded by Sempronius Longus and Servilius Geminus took those of Scipio (Livy 21. 63. 1, Appian *Hann.* 8). One of these legions had been stationed in Cisalpine Gaul in 218 under the command of the praetor Lucius Manlius Vulso. The other had originally been raised for Scipio's expedition to Spain, but was sent instead to Cisalpine Gaul when the Boii rebelled.

[1] For discussion see J. Lazenby, *Hannibal's War* (Warminster, 1978), pp. 33–48, H. Delbrück (trans. W. Renfroe), *History of the Art of War 1* (Nebraska, 1975), pp. 357–362, B. Caven, *The Punic Wars* (London, 1980), pp. 105–6, and J. Peddie, *Hannibal's War* (Gloucestershire, 1997), pp. 100–108.

[2] For a discussion see F. Walbank, *Polybius 1* (Oxford, 1970), pp. 439–440, Lazenby (1978), pp. 75–6 and Delbrück (1971), pp. 325–7. G. de Sanctis, *Storia dei Romani* vol. 3 (Turin-Florence, 1953), ii pp. 131–5 and P. Brunt, *Italian Manpower* (Oxford, 1971), pp. 418–419 argue for the lower figure.

APPENDIX 2: Casualties

A: HANNIBAL'S ARMY

(i) Polybius (3. 117. 6)

- c. 4,000 Gauls, 1,500 Spanish and Africans, and 200 cavalry: Total: 5,700 (11.4% of the army).

(ii) Livy (22. 52. 6)

- c. 8,000 'of his [Hannibal's] bravest men' (16% of the army).

B: THE ROMAN ARMY

(i) Polybius (3. 117. 1–3)

Killed;	c. 70,000 infantry and presumably c. 5,630 cavalry either killed or captured.
Captured:	c. 10,000 infantry
Escaped:	3,000 infantry and 370 cavalry
Total:	**c. 85,630 killed or captured**

Since Polybius gives the Roman strength as 6,000 horse and 80,000 foot before the battle his total of 89,000 for casualties and survivors must be questioned.

(ii) Livy

Killed:	45,500 infantry and 2,700 cavalry (22. 49. 15)
Captured:	3,000 infantry and 1,500 cavalry on the battlefield (22. 49. 19)
	2,000 men who had fled into the ruins of Cannae (22. 49. 13)
	6,400 in the smaller camp (22. 49. 13, 50. 11)
	5,800 in the larger camp (22. 49. 13, 52. 4)
	or 6,400 if Livy included in the total of fugitives from this camp the 600 men led by the tribune Sempronius.
Total prisoners	= 18,700 (or possibly 19,300).

Escaped: 50 with Varro to Venusia immediately after the battle (22. 49. 14)

                4,500 subsequently joined Varro at Venusia (22. 54. 1)

                10,000 to Canusium (22. 54. 4)

Total survivors = 14,550

Sub Totals:

Killed   **= 48,200**

Captured   **= 18,700 (or 19,300)**

Escaped   **= 14,550**

Total   **= 81,450 (or 82,050)**

Livy rounds up the number of dead at Cannae from 48,200 to 50,000 in several speeches (22. 59. 5, 60. 14, 25. 6. 13).

(iii) Other sources:-

(a) Plutarch, Fabius Maximus 16   = 50,000 killed

(b) Appian, Hann. 25   = 50,000 killed

(c) Eutropius 3. 10   = 40,000 infantry and 3,500 cavalry killed

(d) Quintilian 8. 6. 26   = 60,000 killed

C: ROMAN OFFICERS

(i) Known to be with the army:

2 consuls

1 proconsul

2 quaestors

48 tribunes

(ii) Killed:

1 consul   - Lucius Aemilius Paullus (consul 219, 216)

1 proconsul   - Cnaeus Servilius Geminus (consul 217)

2 quaestors   - Lucius Atilius and Lucius Furius Bibaculus

29 tribunes   - including Marcus Minucius Rufus (consul 221)

80 senators   - including some men who were due for enrolment, but had
                  not yet been admitted

(iii) Known survivors:

1 consul	- Caius Terentius Varro (consul 216)
6 (7?) tribunes	- Cnaeus Lentulus
	- Publius Sempronius Tuditanus
	- Quintus Fabius Maximus (consul 213)
	- Lucius Publicius Bibulus
	- Publius Cornelius Scipio (consul 205, 194)
	- Appius Claudius Pulcher (consul 212)

All of these men are named by Livy (22. 49. 6, 50. 6, 53. 1–2). Another tribune, Cnaeus Octavius, is said by the late first century AD source Frontinus to have escaped with Tuditanus (Strategemata 4. 5. 7). If there were eight legions at Cannae and all had their full complement of six tribunes then nineteen survived.

GLOSSARY

ala (pl. *alae*): A contingent supplied for the army by Rome's Italian allies. It had roughly the same number of infantry as a legion, but two to three times as many cavalry.

centurion: The commander of a century in a Roman legion. Some of these men were elected, others appointed to the post.

century: The basic administrative sub-unit of the Roman legion. Each contained from thirty to eighty men and was led by a centurion. There were sixty centuries in each legion.

cohort: The most important sub-unit of an *ala*. The size and internal organization of the cohort are unknown.

consul: Rome's most senior magistrates were the two consuls who held office for a year beginning in March. The consuls were allocated all the most important tasks required by the Republic.

decurion: The commander of a file of ten Roman cavalrymen. There were three decurions in each *turma*.

dictator: In times of crisis the Roman Republic could choose to appoint a single magistrate, or dictator, with supreme power. His term of office was set at six months and could not be renewed.

equites: The highest social and economic class in Roman society, the *equites*, or 'knights', provided the cavalry of the legions.

hastatus (pl. *hastati*): The first line of heavy infantry in the legion, recruited from the younger men.

legion: The most important unit in the Roman army, a legion consisted of cavalry, light infantry, and three lines of close order infantry. There were at least 4,000 foot and 200 horse in each legion, but this number was often increased.

Magister Equitum: The second in command to a dictator.

maniple: The basic tactical unit of the heavy infantry in a legion consisted of two centuries. It was commanded by the centurion of the right-hand maniple if both centurions were present. There were ten maniples in each of the three lines.

optio (pl. *optiones*): The centurion's second in command, the *optio* traditionally stood at the rear of the century.

pilum (pl. *pila*): The heavy javelin which equipped the *hastati* and *principes*.

praetor: The four praetors elected each year were junior to the consuls and held less important military commands, as well as exercising judicial authority.

prefect: Three prefects commanded each *ala*. Their role was probably similar to that of the tribunes in a legion.

princeps (pl. *principes*): The second line of close order infantry in a Roman legion were recruited from men in the prime of life.

quaestor: Junior magistrates who oversaw the Republic's finances and acted as second in command to the consuls.

scutum (pl. *scuta*): A shield, especially the heavy oval body shield carried by Roman legionaries.

socii: The Latin and Italian allies of the Roman Republic. All were obliged to provide men or other support for Roman armies.

suffes (pl. *suffetes*): The two *suffetes* were the senior magistrates of the Carthaginian Republic. However, unlike the Roman consuls, they did not hold military commands. Hannibal was elected *suffes* after the Second Punic War.

triarius (pl. *triarii*): The infantry of the third line of a Roman legion, drawn from the oldest and most experienced soldiers.

tribune: The six tribunes were the senior officers of the legion. Command was held by a pair of tribunes in turn.

turma: The basic tactical unit of the Roman cavalry. It consisted of thirty men, including three decurions.

veles (pl. *velites*): The light infantry of the Roman legion, recruited from the poorest citizens and those too young to serve with the *hastati*.

INDEX

Aegates Islands 22
Aemilianus, Scipio 14, 60
Africa 13, 17, 19, 26–7
   battle 102
   infantry 110–11
   invasion 29
   military system 51
alae 48–9, 83–4, 95–6, 98,
   106
Albinus, Lucius Postumius
   67–8, 169
Alexander the Great 97
Antiochus III, King 24–6
Apollo 166
Appian 15, 96, 121, 126–7
armour 135–6
Atilius, Lucius 155
Aufidius, River 87, 90–3, 95
   aftermath 157
   annihilation 150, 155
   battle 102–3, 147
   encirclement 147
   historical perspective 177,
      180
   opening moves 114

Balearic slingers 51, 53–4, 116
Barcid family 23, 56–7, 169
   see also Hamilcar; Hannibal;
      Hasdrubal
battle
   aftermath 157–76
   annihilation 150–6
   approach 78–9
   armies 191
   battlefield location 86–93
   cavalry clash 118–27
   charge to contact 132–43
   encirclement 143–50
   historical perspective 177–80
   initial deployment 95–113
   opening moves 113–18
   Roman advance 127–32
   see also phases of battle
Bibulus, Lucius 160
Busa 160

caetrati 116
campaign 74–82

Carthage 13–14, 17–40, 50–8,
   169
Carthalo 165, 167
casualties 193–5
Cato the Elder 137
cavalry 43, 49, 54, 57–8
   aftermath 159–60, 162, 165,
      167, 172
   annihilation 150, 152, 154–6
   battle 91–3, 118–27
   campaign 64–5, 80–2
   encirclement 147, 149
   historical perspective 177
   Numidians 145
   Punic 103, 108, 110, 113
   Roman 95–7, 102–3, 106,
      108, 112
Celtiberians 127
Celts 13, 112, 133
   charge 143
   encirclement 147, 149
Centenius, Gaius 37, 95, 98
centurions 44, 46, 49, 140
Cisalpine Gaul 32, 68, 71, 108
Claudius, Appius 160
Connolly, P. 93
consuls 47–9, 60–1, 63–4,
   67–9
   aftermath 160–1, 167, 170
   annihilation 154
   battle 85
   campaign 75, 76, 82
   cavalry 119, 120–1
   encirclement 145
   initial deployment 106
   plan 71

decurions 43, 49
Delbrück, H. 90, 102
deployment 95–113
dictators 37–40, 49, 59, 66
   aftermath 167
   leadership 61
   plan 71–2

Ebro, River 23, 26
Ecnomus, Battle of 112
elephants 33, 53
encirclement 143–50

Ennius 114
Epirus 167
extraordinarii 49, 80

Fabius Maximus, Quintus
   38–40, 59, 66–8
   aftermath 160–1
   annihilation 154–5
   leadership 62–3
   plan of campaign 70–2, 74
First Punic War 19, 26, 28, 38
   campaign 59, 68
   military system 51
   victory 165
Flaminius, Gaius 35, 37–8, 66
   campaign 77
   leadership 60, 62
   Trasimene 85
Forum Boarium 166

Gaesatae 129
Gauls 32, 53–7, 64, 102, 108
   aftermath 157, 169
   annihilation 152, 155
   cavalry 112, 119, 121
   charge to contact 134–6,
      142–3
   encirclement 149
   historical perspective 177
   infantry 110–11
   Roman advance 129–30, 132
Geminus *see* Servilius
   Geminus
Gisgo 77
Gracchus, Tiberius
   Sempronius 167

Hamilcar Barca 22–3, 24–6,
   54, 56, 112
hand-to-hand combat 133–42,
   152–3
Hannibal Barca 9, 11–12
   aftermath 159–70, 172, 176
   annihilation 150, 152–5
   army 189–90, 193
   campaign 59–82
   cavalry 118, 120–1, 125
   character 24–8
   charge to contact 136, 140

encirclement 143, 147–8
historical perspective 177,
   180
invasion 29–36, 38–40, 49
legions 43
marriage 54
military system 51, 53, 56
opening moves 116
Roman advance 127, 132
Saguntum 23–4
tactics 13–14
Hanno 112, 169
Hanson, V.D. 10
Hasdrubal Barca 10, 23, 54,
   56
   aftermath 170
   annihilation 150, 152
   cavalry 119, 125, 126
   encirclement 149
   historical perspective 177
   initial deployment 112
hastati 43–5, 97, 99, 132,
   142–3
Herdonea, Battles of 170, 172
Hollywood 133
hoplites 98, 134
human sacrifice 166

Illyrian War 61, 64
infantry 43–4, 48–9, 53–4
   advance 127–32
   aftermath 159, 172
   annihilation 150, 152, 155,
      156
   cavalry clashes 121, 125,
      126
   charge to contact 132–43
   encirclement 145, 147, 148
   initial deployment 96, 98,
      102
   opening moves 114, 116,
      118–19
   Punic 80, 108, 110
   Roman 64–5, 80, 95, 102–3
initial deployment 95–113
Italy 26–7, 49, 72
   aftermath 163, 166, 169
   campaigns 190–1
   invasion 28–40, 60, 74–5,
      189–90

Josephus 130

Keegan, J. 10
Kromayer, J. 92

Latins 18, 170
leadership 60–4
legions 43–50, 64–70, 72
   aftermath 163, 167, 172
   annihilation 155
   battle 83–4, 91
   encirclement 145–7
   identity 192
   initial deployment 95–8,
      103, 106, 111
   opening moves 116–18
Lehmann, K. 90, 102
Lentulus, Cnaeus 154
Libyans 18, 22, 51, 53
   annihilation 150, 152, 154
   charge to contact 136
   deployment 110–13
   encirclement 148–9
   historical perspective 177
   military system 56
   opening moves 116
Ligurians 51, 64
Livy 14–15, 40, 43, 61–2
   aftermath 159–62, 167, 169
   annihilation 154–5
   battle 83, 85
   campaign 65–7, 75–6
   cavalry 118–21, 125–6
   charge to contact 142
   initial deployment 95, 112
   plan 70–2
location of battlefield 86–93

Macedonian Wars 14, 172
Magister Equitum 37, 67, 155,
   167
magistrates 47–9, 51, 60, 68,
   167
Mago Barca 112, 140, 152,
   169–70
Maharbal 112, 162
maniples 44–6, 83, 97–102
   annihilation 150, 152
   battle 110, 127
   charge to contact 143
   encirclement 145, 147–8
   historical perspective 177
Marcellus, Marcus Claudius
   67–8, 166–7
Master of Horse 37–9, 67,
   155, 167
Matho, Marcus Pomponius 67
Mercenary War 22, 51
Metellus, Marcus Caecilius
   160
Minucius Rufus, Marcus

38–40, 49, 61–2, 66–7, 155
Monomachus, Hannibal 28
Montgomery, B.L. 162

naval forces 27–8
Numidians 51, 53–4, 82, 85
   aftermath 159, 172
   battle 93, 108, 112
   cavalry 120, 126
   encirclement 145, 149
   opening moves 116

Octavius, Cnaeus 159
optiones 44, 101, 140

Paullus, Lucius Aemilius 10,
   60–4, 70–1
   aftermath 165
   annihilation 152, 154–5
   battle 84
   battlefield location 92
   campaign 74, 77, 80–2
   cavalry 119–20, 125–6
   charge to contact 140
   encirclement 145
   initial deployment 95–6,
      103, 113
Pera, Marcus Junius 167
phalanxes 37, 148, 149
phases of battle
   first 116–21
   second 124–40
   third 140–7
   fourth 147–50
   fifth 150–6
Philip V, King 172
Philus, Publius Furius 67, 160
Phoenicians 17
Pictor, Fabius 166
pila 44–5, 53–4, 100, 130–2,
   136
plan of campaign 70–4
Plutarch 14–15, 71, 120
Polybius 10, 14–15, 24, 28
   aftermath 160, 162
   annihilation 154–5
   battle 84–5
   battlefield location 87, 90,
      93
   campaign 64–5, 74–6, 82
   cavalry 119, 120
   charge to contact 142
   deployment 95–7, 99, 103,
      110, 112
   encirclement 147
   invasion 33

military system 43, 45, 49,
53, 70
patron 60–1
plan 70, 72
Roman advance 127, 131
praetors 49, 67, 166, 169
prefects 48–9, 84, 106, 143
principes 43–4, 97–9
Pyrrhus, King 167

quincunx formation 10, 45

Regulus, Marcus Atilius 40,
75–6
Romans 13–15, 37
advance 127–32
army 191–5
delay 37–40
Hannibal 24–8
invasion 28–37
military system 41–50
opening moves 116
Rommel, E. 180

Saguntum 23–4, 163
Salinator, Marcus Livius 61
Sardinia 17, 22, 27
Schwartzkopf, N. 9, 180
Scipio, Publius Cornelius
29–33, 36, 49, 66
aftermath 160, 172
leadership 60
scorched earth policy 71
scuta 44, 131
Second Punic War 14–15,
22–4, 26
aftermath 165, 176
campaign 74
cavalry 120, 125
charge to contact 137
military system 50
opening moves 114, 116
Seleucids 24
Sempronius Longus, Titus 29,
32–3, 66
battle 85
invasion 36
military system 49
Senate 29, 32, 35, 60–1
aftermath 161, 166–8, 172
annihilation 155
campaign 67, 70, 75
leadership 63–4
military system 49
Servilius Geminus, Cnaeus 35,
37–8, 40

annihilation 152, 155
campaign 60, 66, 75–6
charge to contact 140
encirclement 145
initial deployment 103, 106
Sicily 17, 19, 22, 26–7
aftermath 166, 172
campaign 60, 68
invasion 29, 32
signifer 44
skirmishers 114–16, 145
Punic 53–4, 110
Roman 45, 98, 127
Southern Gaul 29
Spaniards 13, 17, 23–6
aftermath 172
annihilation 152
caetrati 116
campaign 60
cavalry 108, 112, 119, 121
charge to contact 133–6,
142–3
encirclement 147, 149
historical perspective 177
infantry 110–11
invasion 28–9, 32
military system 51, 53–4
Roman advance 129–30, 132
speirai 110
Sybilline Books 166

Telamon, Battle of 64, 116,
130, 142
tesseratius 44
Third Punic War 14
Ticinus, Battle of 120, 126,
172
Trasimene, Battle of 36–8, 40,
53
aftermath 161, 163
armies 191
campaign 59, 66, 70
comparison 85, 153
deployment 102
equipment 148
Trebia, Battle of 33–5, 49, 53
aftermath 161
armies 190–1
campaign 59–60, 66, 70
cavalry 118, 126
comparison 85, 91, 93
deployment 102
equipment 148
experimentation 112
infantry 111
military system 57

skirmishers 110
triarii 44–5, 96, 98–100, 150
tribunes 46–7, 49, 66–7
aftermath 159, 160
annihilation 152, 155
battle 84
charge to contact 140, 143
initial deployment 106
opening moves 113
triplex acies 97, 101
Tuditanus, Publius Sempronius
159–60
turmae 43, 49

Varro, Caius Terentius 10,
60–4
aftermath 160–1, 166–7
annihilation 150, 155
battle 83–5
battlefield location 92–3
campaign 75–6, 80, 82
cavalry 126
encirclement 143, 145, 149
initial deployment 96–7,
103, 106, 108
plan 68, 70–1
Veith, G. 92
velites 45, 80, 98, 108
annihilation 150
battle 116, 118–19
Vestal Virgins 166
victory 161–8
Volturnus 90
Von Schlieffen, A. 9, 180

Zama, Battle of 111, 172, 176

PICTURE CREDITS